NEW TEACHERS IN AN URBAN COMPREHENSIVE SCHOOL
LEARNING IN PARTNERSHIP

Edited by Ruth Heilbronn and Crispin Jones

Trentham Books

First published in 1997 by Trentham Books Limited

Trentham Books Limited
Westview House
734 London Road
Oakhill
Stoke on Trent
Staffordshire
England ST4 5NP

British Cataloguing in Publication Data
A catalogue record for this book is available from the British Library
ISBN: 1 85856 056 X

Designed and typeset by Trentham Print Design Ltd., Chester
and printed in Great Britain by The Cromwell Press Ltd., Wiltshire.

NEW TEACHERS IN AN URBAN COMPREHENSIVE SCHOOL
LEARNING IN PARTNERSHIP

CONTENTS

Section Three. Training in its Wider Context

Appendices

ACKNOWLEDGEMENTS

The editors would like to thank all their contributors. Caught up in the hectic world of teaching, all gave generously of their time towards this project. Particular thanks are also due to Athe Demetriades, Peter Fenn, Lilah Heilbronn, Edna-Mairi Heilbronn, Andy Hudson, Jean Jones, Sheila Kasobova, Karen Leaney, Maurice Oliphant, Ben Moore and Amanda Stone.

INTRODUCTION

Sixty per cent of all teacher training and education became school-based during the years 1992-96 and partnerships were established between schools and higher education institutions. This is a case study based on one London comprehensive school's response to these changes and it illuminates the interests and concerns of all involved in initial teacher training and education (ITET).

The effect of increasing school-based time to two thirds of all training has been enormous. The 'training context' has now become a crucial factor in the initial training and education of teachers. Whether the school has a selective intake, is grant maintained, single-sex, denominational or secular can have a marked influence on the beginning teachers' earliest training. Location and setting are also important. A beginning teacher trained in rural Devon, for example, will meet a different set of local issues from counterparts in an urban school in Birmingham. Nevertheless certain core issues and concerns remain across all these contexts. The key issue is the beginning teachers' entitlement to good quality training and support in their placement schools. This book details some processes and strategies which have been effective in creating a good training context and which we think can apply to any placement school.

We have divided the book into three sections:

Section One is called *The Whole School Context* and in Chapter 1 we map out the range of issues raised throughout the book. In Chapter 2, the Head discusses her vision of the whole school as a learning community, which makes learning to teach a part of the general ethos of the learning school. (To contextualise the school we have given more detailed data about it in Appendix 1.) Chapter 3 gives an overview of the new role of the school-based tutor in setting up systems to nurture, coordinate and monitor training. Chapters 4-7 describe how the school informs and educates its beginning teachers about a range of key issues: special educational needs and its statutory provision; the support of bilingual students who are using English as an additional language; Information Technology and the current expectations for learning in an information rich future, and a current major concern at Hampstead School, the provision of an appropriate education for its many refugee students. These cross-curricular concerns face all teachers, including beginning teachers who wish to work in urban schools in Britain, and all the chapters contain useful information, guidance and tips.

Section Two: *Individuals Learning* illustrates for beginning teachers, mentors and higher education partners how the 'training context' can be used both to create subject competence and for wider professional studies. Chapter 8, for example, shows how school-based research can benefit the beginning teacher by offering contextualized information and data about specific aspects of educational practice. Such research can be a spring-board for further study and it can also enable beginning teachers to relate theory to practice in a direct and relevant way. Chapters 9 and 10 describe the work of two departmental subject supervisors mentoring their beginning teachers. They are written by Maths and Science teachers but will be of interest to people working in *all* curriculum areas, since they describe the process of mentoring, through the eyes of two experienced and successful trainers. They give the school 'training context' since they follow the same procedures as all other curriculum areas in the school. That the process has been successful is proved by the permanent appointments the school has made from the ranks of its beginning teachers.

Section Three: *Training in its Wider Context* moves out to the wider perspective of training and in-service development. Chapter 11 describes the contribution made by higher education to training subject supervisors/mentors within school. Clearly the mentor role is crucial: mentors have a major responsibility for ensuring that their beginning teachers become competent to carry out all the functions of a teacher of that curriculum subject. The chapter describes building structures through which mentors in school can 'articulate their practice', reflect and analyse, so that they can present their experience appropriately to their beginning teachers (BTs). This detailed study of the development of mentor training gives a full picture of the Higher Education Institution's support to the school in this area.

Chapter 12 describes the work of the local education authority in bringing together a variety of provision, linking higher education with the in-service training of qualified teachers and with the teacher tutors of newly qualified teachers, i.e. teachers in their second year of training, who have already achieved qualified teacher status. The chapter demonstrates the importance of the local authority to the school in ensuring consistency throughout these two initial years and gives detailed background to developments in training in the UK over the past few years. The book ends by situating the school in its contemporary, urban setting. Chapter 13 gives background information on education in London and relates work described in other chapters, such as Chapter 6, on the education of bilingual learners, to a wider canvas, placing developments here in their broad social and political context, as we believe teacher education and training should always do.

NOTES ON CONTRIBUTORS

Jonathan Bach was Head of Science at Hampstead School for six years, and has an interest in mentoring and professional development of teachers. He is now Deputy Headteacher of Preston Manor School.

Leon Gore is Initial Training and Induction Co-ordinator for Camden LEA and is responsible for the LEA's primary and secondary induction programmes for newly qualified teachers. He is an active member of the London Induction Co-ordinators Group, has been an advisory teacher, and a head of department in a secondary school.

Ruth Heilbronn is a senior teacher at Hampstead School, where she teaches French and Spanish. She has worked in the area of professional development for a number of years and is a co-tutor for the PGCE course at the Institute of Education, University of London.

Tamsyn Imison has been Headteacher of Hampstead School since September 1984. She is on the Executive Committee of the Secondary Heads' Association and has a strong commitment to the 'Learning School'. She was involved in the pilot ITET group with Pat Ashton at Leicester and was on the DES INSET steering group.

Crispin Jones is a senior lecturer in the Culture, Communication and Societies Group at the Institute of Education, University of London, where he mainly works in the area of inter-cultural education. He has been involved with ITET at Hampstead School for a number of years.

Pat Mikhail is the special needs co-ordinator (SENCO) at Hampstead School and is also in charge of primary liaison. She regularly gives INSET to teachers on the area of special educational needs provision and curriculum support.

Cathy Pomphrey is a senior lecturer in Education at the University of North London, where she is course tutor to the PGCE Modern Languages. She was previously a head of department and senior teacher at Hampstead School.

Phil Taylor is the Director of Information Technology at Hampstead School. He has worked in the field of educational computing for seven years including a period with the Institute of Education's Computing Service.

Margaret Tettey is deputy head of Mathematics at Hampstead School. She has worked closely with B.Ed beginning teachers from the University of North London for the past five years and has been a mentor with responsibility for the assessment of block practices for the past two years.

Marc Thompson is head of Bilingual Support at Hampstead School. He has worked widely in the field of curriculum support, in England and abroad, as an ESL teacher, and SEN support teacher and individual support teacher for statemented children.

GLOSSARY OF EDUCATIONAL TERMS

Education has a jargon of its own, which changes rapidly, particularly given the disruption and reforms that education has been subjected to over the last decade.

In this text the following terms are used freely and may need some explanation.

ATL	Association of Teachers and Lecturers. A teacher and lecturer union
B.Ed	Four year teacher education and training course
BT, BTs	Beginning teachers. These are people training to become teachers, usually through one of two routes, the PGCE or the B.Ed. Traditionally called student teachers or just 'students'
CLASS	Camden Language Support Service
DES	Department of Education and Science. The title of the English Ministry of Education until succeeded by:
DFE	The Department for Education. The title of the English Ministry of Education until succeeded by:
DFEE	The Department for Education and Employment
ESL, E2L, EAL	English as a second or additional language
ESN	Educational special needs. Refers to school students who have special learning needs. The member of staff with responsibility for this area of a school's work is referred to as SENCO, or special educational needs co-ordinator
ESW	Educational Social Worker, formerly EWO or Educational Welfare Officer. A sort of educational paramedic, dealing with school student welfare and attendance issues
GCSE	General Certificate in Secondary Education. National examination normally taken at age 16
GEST	Grants for Educational Support and Training given by central government for specific work in designated areas, e.g. school improvement
GNVQ	General National Vocational Qualification. Vocational courses usually taken after the end of compulsory schooling, i.e. post 16 years of age
HE	Higher Education
HEI	Higher Education Institution

HMI	Her Majesty's Inspector(ate) of Schools
HOD	Head of Department. Teacher responsible for subject curriculum area or areas
HOY	Head of Year. Usually a pastoral role. In some secondary schools, the same role is undertaken by House Heads, a vertical pastoral grouping
IEP	Individual Education Plan: an educational work/development plan for a child with special educational needs
ILEA	Inner London Education Authority. Unitary authority for central London, abolished in 1991
INSET	In service education and training
IST	Individual Support Teacher
ITE	Initial Teacher Education
ITET	Initial Teacher Education and Training. The term preferred in this book, although all three terms [ITE, ITET and ITT] are used
ITT	Initial Teacher Training
KS3, KS4	Key Stages in the secondary schools for assessing academic attainment at National Curriculum Levels. KS3 is assessed by SATs and KS4 by the GCSE
LEA	Local Education Authority. Statutory body responsible for schools in a borough or other local government area
LMS	Local management of schools. Refers to range of measures designed to give greater financial autonomy to schools
MFL	Modern Foreign Languages
NAS/UWT	National Association of Schoolmasters/Union of Women Teachers. A teacher union
NUT	National Union of Teachers. Another teacher union
NQT	Newly qualified teacher, in their first year of work in a school after qualifying
Ofsted	Office for Standards in Education
PGCE	Postgraduate Certificate in Education. One year postgraduate course in education
PSE/PSH	Personal and Social Education/ Personal, Social and Health Education. Often taught as part of the pastoral work of schools
QTS	Qualified Teacher Status
SATS	Standard Attainment Tests. National tests of attainment. In secondary schools, these are at age 14 and 16, Key Stage 3 and Key Stage 4. Key Stage 4 is assessed currently by the GCSE
SCAA	The School Curriculum and Assessment Authority. Government quango responsible for the National Curriculum and its assessment during this period

Section 11	Funding Central government money given to fund ESL or bilingual support teaching (and a few other programmes designed to help ethnic minorities) in schools and LEAs. Now being phased out by the SRB (q.v.)
Senior Executive	Senior management team of Hampstead School, consisting of the Head, three deputies and three senior teachers
SHA	Secondary Heads Association. Headteachers' trade union
SRB	Single Regeneration Budget. Extra funds given by central government to disadvantaged areas, usually inner city ones
Stages 1, 2, 3 and 4	Stages of English proficiency for ESL/EAL bilingual school students. Stage 1 is low competence, 4 is high
Statement	A Statement of Special Educational Needs is a formal document resulting from LEA/school processes of assessment. The school students with such Statements have become known as 'statemented' school students
SEN	Special educational needs
SENCO	A school's special educational needs' co-ordinator
TES	*Times Educational Supplement*
THES	*Times Higher Educational Supplement*
TTA	Teacher Training Agency. Government quango responsible for teacher training/education

SECTION ONE:
THE WHOLE SCHOOL CONTEXT

CHAPTER 1

THEMES AND ISSUES

Ruth Heilbronn

The Background

This case study covers the years 1992-96, a time of development and change in teacher training, heralded by the publication of two government circulars (DFE, 1992 and DFE, 1993a). Change was far-reaching, requiring reorganising the content and the management of courses of initial teacher training, more training time in schools and less in university departments of education, and competence-based assessment was introduced. The circulars raised important questions, particularly about the role of universities in teacher education and what has been called a 'radical reconceptualisation of current practice' (Wideen and Grimmett, 1995, p. 202). In the debate and controversy which raged during the years leading up to the introduction of the new courses, in the academic year 1994/95, it some-times appeared from school level that teacher education was 'more in a state of turmoil... than in a state of continuous improvement' (Op.cit. p. 202).

Underlying the shift of placement time to schools has been the issue of funding, as schools have gained more training resources. Neither Higher Education Institutions (HEI) nor schools believe that they have enough resources to do the job as thoroughly as they wish.

> Control of funding has been a powerful weapon for the current government in ensuring the policy influences practice. Yet that power will always be limited by the 'slippage' that separates policy and practice (McBride 1996, pg. 2).

To see in detail how a school has marshalled these resources is to understand something about the whole learning climate in that school, as it affects all teachers, beginning teachers (BTs) and school students. In fact the school had already been involved in training teachers from a number of higher education institutions and therefore found itself in the midst of the debate on the establish-ment of partnerships with higher education, the development of teacher com-petences and the link between the various phases of professional development.

Good Teachers

Our first training objective is to produce good teachers, competent and skilled practitioners who are well prepared to teach a diverse school student population. 'This means that teacher educators must teach teachers 'to build on the cultural experiences that children bring to school, using those experiences to create moments of positive learning.' (Mary Hatwood Futrell, in Kaplan and Edelfelt, 1996, p. 14). The particular context of Hampstead school as an urban comprehensive is of importance in understanding this underlying principle and emerges clearly throughout the book.

Beginning teachers need to understand the individual needs of their pupils and to develop a holistic comprehension of their own future role and place in school. This will be the foundation on which to build their lessons, since they will apply their general subject knowledge to prepare lessons for *particular* classes and groups. The most crucial factor in their development is their growing ability to relate theory to practice – and time is tight, particularly on PGCE courses. A fine balance needs to be struck between information gathered in readings and lectures, and practice based learning. How courses mould this theory/practice balance is crucial. We pondered about whether we were writing a book about initial teacher training or initial teacher education. We thought that the specific skills and competences required of a teacher were best described by the word 'training', rather like the use of the term to describe specific medical skills, e.g. we thought that we would not care whether a surgeon operating on us was educated or not, but we would worry if he was not trained. Then we realised that we had entered into the competences debate which has raged over the past few years. Finally we understood that we valued both aspects and we have decided to use the term ITET to cover initial teacher education and training.

ITET is a complex interweaving of many elements. Competence-based assessment certainly anchors the whole structure. At Hampstead, part of the whole school context must be our attitude to learning and our understanding of the processes involved. For example we recently revised our school assessment policy as we wanted the principles on which it was based to be clear and transparent to all. Therefore we value the consistency and clarity which a competence-based approach has given us. In our work with beginning teachers we were also concerned that too narrow a definition of the competences would not fit our ITET aims because we might be trying to break down what is complex into over-restrictive performance criteria and performance indicators. We had seen from the our involvement with GNVQ assessment, how much evidence had to be amassed to verify the criteria. We knew that the move to competence-based assessment was based on the belief that educational theory should be taught in relation to practice and not divorced from it. The question of whether theory has been too undervalued by the emphasis on the practical elements of the courses still remains open. Some theorists expressed grave doubts about the whole competence-based approach (see particularly Rieck, 1992; Burke, 1989; Carr, 1993a and 1993b).

Reading through this book will reveal that our contributors do not follow a purely mechanistic model of training, in which competences may be ticked off until qualified teacher status is attained. They do accept, of course, that learning to teach successfully in a curriculum area is fundamental to teacher training. Lesson planning, classroom management, subject knowledge and application are of fundamental importance and no beginning teacher will be given qualified teacher status if they are weak in these areas. All the contributors to this book also believe in providing opportunities for beginning teachers to develop as all-round practitioners, whilst fulfilling their primary training objective to develop teaching competence across a broad range.

In addition, Hampstead School is committed to encouraging beginning teachers to reflect on their practice. Tamsyn Imison states, in Chapter 2, that the key strategy must be to develop teams of reflective learners. The school's work with these teams represents a commitment to reflective practice and to 'the joys and pains of close attention to the intuitive thinking revealed in the very particular phenomena of actual performance' (Schön, 1983 p. ix). All the ITET courses with which the school is involved value this model of learning, teaching and practice. The arguments about the importance of reflection on the wider role of the teacher have apparently become more acceptable to current policy makers. Referring to current proposals to develop a national standard for continuous professional development, across a teacher's career, the chief executive of the Teacher Training Agency has assured practitioners and trainers alike that 'it is possible and necessary to be explicit, without resorting to a string of reductionist competences' (Gardiner, 1996b).

BTs at the school undertake several tasks to develop their abilities to reflect on their experiences in teaching and learning and to identify targets for development, a subject taken up later in the book by subject supervisors/ mentors, who outline this process. Effective and supportive training cannot take place in just one department in isolation or in a higher education institution where elements of the course do not merge harmoniously. The whole course climate is important (see also Jones J., 1994 and Salmon, 1980).

Through their research tasks, too, BTs gain understanding of the wider educational context. In their school-based assignments, described in Chapter 3 and 8, the BT as researcher is required to study the theory and research findings which underpin an area of educational policy or practice they have identified to produce a final piece of assessed, written work. BTs are welcome in school for the freshness they bring to teaching, the fact that they make us reflect on our own work as teachers and because as researchers, they may work on a task which also benefits the school. We can guide and direct the BT into an area in which we have expertise, which can also be one in which we may wish to develop. The BT can help us by undertaking research tasks with us, thus contributing to an already developing area of school practice. An example of an IT survey which served this purpose is given Chapter 5.

ITET consists then of a series of processes with which the beginning teachers engage, involving a nexus of relationships within which they meet a mixture of formal tasks, information to be digested and practical problems. This book presents aspects, features, examples of these processes and shows the range of experiences provided by this particular school, in its urban context. Together they form a picture of a complex learning situation opened up to beginning teachers, on which they need to reflect as they develop in their practice. Simply applying *subject knowledge* does not make a good teacher. In training teachers we are not merely grooming appliers of subject knowledge. Much more is involved.

Good mentors

This book shows that being a good practitioner is inextricably bound up with the quality of support given to that practitioner. No individual, however talented and hardworking, can be a good teacher in a school which does not support and guide them appropriately. A large amount of technical information needs to be learnt and practised. Specific subject knowledge needs to be applied. Beginning teachers have to learn to draw out what needs to be taught in a particular context, namely the particular groups of school students which they face and their *individual* learning needs. Understanding the context and applying subject knowledge learnt in their first degree or on theoretical courses, requires clear analysis on the part of the trainer and much work from the beginning teacher. It is the foundation of all other aspects of learning how to be a good teacher.

The mentors' role is crucial: without good mentors the beginning teacher cannot develop and flourish. Therefore, in providing this case study we have tried to show what makes a good teacher educator. Mentors however, are teachers in a school. They have roles and responsibilities in curriculum departments. Their training and development must also be addressed as the bedrock of their work. The quality of the support they are given will depend on a complex variety of factors, beginning with the values of the school, on its management structure and effectiveness and the quality and attitude of its staff in the wider sense, which includes all support staff.

The learning school ethos encompasses the idea of education as a life-long process. What is initiated in the year leading up to gaining qualified teacher status (QTS) continues through the newly qualified stage and links to in-service training and further professional development. Indeed, proposals for a national standard to accredit these phases is currently under development (TTA: 1996). Mentor training, 'articulating practice' (see Chapter 11), therefore adds to the effectiveness and the development of the teachers lucky enough to participate. It also spreads across to others, if it is well coordinated and monitored.

To pass or to fail?

The problem of the BT who is unable to make the grade is an abiding issue, dealt with by several contributors. We believe that much that is pertinent to being a good teacher can be taught. But there are other factors, more difficult to teach, that depend on the beginning teachers' personal qualities and circumstances. Evidently the initial interview needs to pick realistically among applicants who can show the qualities and dispositions which will enable them to gain the skills to become good teachers. At the time of writing there is a shortage of applicants in certain subjects, such as Maths and Modern Languages and there are indications that pressure may be exerted to have entry qualifications lowered. We believe it would be unwise to lower entry demands, both for formal qualifications and for personal suitability as gauged at an interview. Great pressure is also put on schools by unsuitable candidates. There are also occasions when a beginning teacher who has given every indication of succeeding, starts to give cause for concern while on teaching practice, requiring counselling and much liaison between the parties involved.

Partnership between school and higher education

Partnership has emerged as a keyword in public discourse during the period covered by this case study. It has become almost a cliché, yet it has a particular significance in the ITET context. It implies that what is needed to create, nurture and maintain a good learning institution is the effective and targeted support of many people, from higher education institutions and from schools, working together. The individual contributions in this book build up a picture of this nexus of support.

'Joint responsibility for the planning and management of courses and the selection, training and assessment of students has been envisaged' (DFE, 1992, paragraph 14). In establishing this new basis for teacher training, the Department for Education stated that the balance of responsibilities for the new courses would vary between institutions, although it laid down that schools would have 'a leading responsibility for training students to teach their specialist subject, to assess students and to manage classes; and for supervising students and assessing their competence in these respects' and that higher education institutions would be responsible 'for ensuring these courses meet the requirements for academic validation, presenting courses for accreditation, awarding qualifications to successful students and arranging student placements in more than one school'. It was left to the parties involved in these partnership arrangements to work our how these aspects of training would be divided and how cohesion would be achieved.

Partnership is a strong thread running through this book. Mentors speak of their pleasure at extending their skills and participating in university planning; partnership with the local authority is clearly important, as is school-based research. However, funding remains a problem. Higher education institutions have less of the funding for training than before the new arrangements, as they pass more of the funding to schools. So higher education tutors visit their BTs less often while they are on practice placements, possibly only once per term. Consequently, tutors in school have a growing role in the assessment of beginning teachers. Teachers also participate in interviewing candidates for courses in partnership institutions. Responsible for assessments, supporting school-based research, mentoring and supervising professional studies, schools which are successful in training believe they have developed their own training practice, to the advantage of the school's general effectiveness. So we bear the workload for these overall benefits. However, funding remains a recurrent issue, as is evident in the book.

Conclusion

Wide concern has been expressed that increasing time spent in school would lead to poorer quality training. The book is the result of our conviction that it is possible to maintain a sound training base within the new requirements. It is a case study which develops also the argument for a community of learners, supported by effective partnership arrangements and based on the philosophy of continual professional development. This development needs to be founded on a rigorous system of support for the practice based elements, and a respect for the place of theory, research and reflection.

CHAPTER 2

HAMPSTEAD SCHOOL AS A LEARNING COMMUNITY

Tamsyn Imison

Teaching is not to be regarded as a static accomplishment like riding a bicycle or keeping a ledger; it is, like all arts of high ambition, a strategy in the face of an impossible task. (Stenhouse, 1983, p.189)

I started my Headship at Hampstead in 1984, at a time when the school roll was just over a thousand, examination results were below the London average, only 30% of school students were staying on into a selective sixth-form and few members of staff felt it necessary to be involved in staff development. The gender and age profile of the staff was very different from the present one. Only two substantive heads of department were women and these were in the 'traditional' women's roles in Home Economics and Business Studies. Until my appointment all the top eight posts in the school had been held by men and my appointment was a gender shock for the whole institution. In addition, the ethos regarding new-comers and new ideas was very different from now; for example, after completing ten years in post, a member of staff was eligible to belong to the exclusive 'veterans club' of the school. I found that the environment of the school needed attention: graffiti and vandalism were everywhere and the school looked uncared for and run down. Teamwork approaches were the exception not the rule and whole school development was at a virtual standstill. There were no computers in the school.

Within a term we were into intense industrial action and massively reducing resources, as the ILEA struggled against rate-capping and political attack. We were teaching groups of thirty in all subject areas and there were no extra-curricular activities. The only consultation was with parents through the Head's Open Door (attendance figures of over 100 were quite common), and with school students. One notable Year 10 assembly, when I set out for the school students what I hoped to do in the school, lasted all morning. Unfortunately, no staff were present! Despite the continuing austerity, things began to change. Staff were encouraged and new, enthusiastic colleagues joined them. A positive team spirit emerged and growth across the whole school became visible. This is the context I would like to explore in this chapter, the idea of an institution where everyone – the school students and the adults around them – is learning.

Hampstead School: 'Cricklewood High' in 1996

Hampstead School is a true comprehensive, with 1,279 school students and 81 teachers. It draws from the full range of attainment, with 25% in the top, 25% in the bottom reading bands and 50% in the centre band. There is a good social and ethnic mix and there also a balance in most years between girls and boys. The name of the school is very misleading, as most of our intake comes from Cricklewood and Kilburn, which are inner-city areas, and not from leafy Hampstead, a few miles away. (More details of the school are given in Appendix 1, where material collected for a recent Ofsted inspection of the school is given. Presented here are a few of the more salient characteristics of the school.) Fifty-five percent of the students are bilingual or multilingual, speaking over eighty different languages between them. This includes about 150 asylum seekers, whose high motivation rubs off on others and who also help to make Hampstead an international secondary school. On LEA raw and value-added comparative analysis, our school delivers high SATs, GCSE and A Level examination results, has high attendance and low exclusion rates and many school students stay on for after-school activities. Girls do particularly well and boys' performance has recently moved up to match it. Of the Year 11 cohort, virtually 100% have been staying on into post-16 education and training, for the last five years. There are 230 school students in our own sixth form, which is currently capped at that level because of serious space constraints.

In terms of training and development for teachers and support staff, our staff profile shows a majority of high attaining, strongly committed colleagues, with women and people from ethnic minorities well represented in senior positions. Many expect to move on to further promotion or development, while a significant number are studying or have studied for further degrees. They act as excellent role models for other staff and school students.

Our management structure allows for participation in decision-making throughout the school, so we have task groups open to every member of staff to advise on major policy decisions and a senior executive team of seven who work together as a group on all areas of management. This also provides opportunities for development within the senior team, as information is shared and jobs rotated.

Our aims as a school are set out in the following statement of intent, which is regularly revised by staff, governors, parents and school students. The most significant thing about our aims is that we consider everyone to be part of the learning community:

Fig.2. 1.

Learning together, achieving together

At Hampstead School everyone will strive to :

– enjoy the challenges and achievement of learning

– develop individual strengths

– experience academic, social and personal success

– manage setbacks

– develop consideration and co-operation within a stimulating and supportive environment and with the support of family and the wider community.

The Ofsted Inspectors told us in May 1996 that Hampstead School was a good school because of the quality of the teaching. This was the best thing we could have been told. I am sure we have achieved this because we are a 'learning' institution. Furthermore, if we are to develop teaching as an art we have to focus on outcomes and the successful outcome we have all agreed is for all of us to be learning. This communicates across the whole institution making it, as an excellent headteacher once said, '*a learning hive*'. We deploy many strategies to bring this about, but the key strategy must be to develop teams of reflective learners. The bigger and broader the team, the more exciting the learning. Involving beginning teachers and higher education colleagues has this effect. As a member of the DES Initial Teacher INSET Steering Group in 1981/3 and the Tutor Coordinator piloting this in a large comprehensive school in South East London, I saw for myself how this model of joint teams, focusing on both curriculum development and the training of beginning teachers, could work. It was an exciting way of setting up mutual support and development, as the beginning teachers were well supported within a stimulating team, who were also all learning; they immediately found themselves talking about good teaching and ways of improving their practice.

The new, more balanced partnership between schools and higher education is ready made to set up this kind of collaboration. It has other benefits, as it prevents those in higher education being de-skilled as practitioners and gives opportunities for the classroom teacher to reflect and develop good practice. So the beginning teacher benefits, the teacher and department team benefit and, most importantly, the school students benefit, because the outcome is likely to improve or at least support good teaching and learning. By including beginning teachers and higher education partners in these teams we have greater scope because these 'interested others' may have a less insular and, in the case of those in HE, broader perspective.

The school as a learning institution

As we approach the 21st century we need new approaches to teaching and learning. If we are to be successful in raising the achievement levels of everyone, including the school students who find it hardest, we must enlist the active support of all partners in education – our school students, their parents, colleagues, support specialists, industry and community mentors, as well as beginning teachers, higher education partners and researchers. We must use a whole armament of strategies, including new partnerships and new technologies, for managing learning. We must establish true learning centres where adults and school students learn together. The rigid boundaries existing around institutions, curricula, day and year structures will have to be changed and time found for daily conversations, preparation, assessment and evaluation, to support the action plans of each learner, school students and teachers, so that everyone can develop, reflect and plan their next steps forward. Using extended teams that include HE partners and beginning teachers will be very productive in this regard.

Additionally, action research can be a reflective evaluation tool, a point explored further in Chapter 8. Stenhouse (1985) put forward the case for research as the basis for teaching

> research gains accrue from the gradual accumulation of knowledge through the patient definition of error .... a decade of inservice education which neglects curriculum research ... will be wasting the greatest potential of an immense investment.

The opportunity for such action research, using everyone involved in initial teacher training, is immense. My first personal experience of this was on the Steering Group for Pat Ashton's initial training INSET in Leicester in 1982, where I observed a Maths department team which included beginning teachers and HE tutors working alongside the classroom teacher and others in the department, in a Leicestershire comprehensive school. This clearly showed the value of team observation, evaluation and planning, to introduce curriculum development and better practice in respect of equal opportunities. It was really exciting and it allowed the beginning teachers to access higher order thinking and planning. What was also particularly pleasing was to see the HE lecturers teaching alongside the beginning teachers.

The necessity for these links across the spectrum of education is constant. For example, an eye opener for me was discovering the ideas of Vygotsky, Bruner and Glasersfeld last year while studying for my Open University MA. I recognised their vision of learning as a true dialogue with others. I was captivated by the concept of the zone of proximal development – the region between what we know and what we want to know, and the idea of scaffolding and navigation. It clarifies my views and strategies as a practitioner for supporting timid learners, helps me to understand my own learning and articulate this more clearly with colleagues.

Learning Across the School

John Dewey, in *Democracy and Education*, said that society not only existed by transmission and by communication but that it existed in transmission and communication. We are trying at Hampstead to engage in learning that comes from talking and debating together in search of common understandings. In this, we are supporting the Piagetian legacy of respect for children's capacities as learners, as makers of their own understanding and as capable of self-correction and instruction. Our experience is that if all teachers and pupils are valued, their training and courses made high status by involving industrialists and others from the community, they become very proud of their work, their motivation increases and they become actively involved in their own learning and progression. If this leads the weakest school students on to another relevant, practically-based course requiring independent learning, they are more likely to become confident, mature adults, who value learning.

I describe learners as those confident enough or valued and supported enough to engage in real dialogues about learning. I am thinking of Vygotsky's ideas of co-operation with others and Bruner's view that 'the problem is not with competence but with performance' and that learning is amenable to improvement, so that we can be taught how to learn. This is vital and teachers who are also learners are best equipped to support learning strategies. I think good teachers are those who have been made to feel that they succeed in their own learning.

It follows that teachers should be seen as supportive positive adult learners, who are prepared to understand and identify the needs of all school students and share with them the excitement of travelling from the known to the unknown; who prepare guides, maps and charts, scaffolding and dictionaries to make sense for the school student of the path they are following, the knowledge, skills and understanding they are accessing and the purpose of it all.

The qualities needed to do this reflect our statement of intent, namely, that teachers have certain essential qualities:

- they like and value young people; have very high expectations for all of them and are prepared to help them become independent learners

- they have not lost the zest for learning and discovery and can communicate it to others

- they continue to search for proficiency with others, in their own area of expertise.

In addition, teachers need to be communicators, strategists and evaluators. This can be summed up as follows:

1. Teachers as communicators

A good teacher:

- is sensitive to and responds to group dynamics

- uses relevant, jargon-free language and has an awareness of the importance of language in communication and will listen without interrupting or putting words into others' mouths

- is aware of and uses to effect the classroom environment and presents things well

- is a bit of a performer who knows the value of surprise and fun.

2. Teachers as strategists

A good teacher:

- is patient and enjoys helping

- understands school students' needs and access points for learning

- is open to others and helps them play a forward role

- is a good manager

- instinctively maps the territory

- is good at preparation

- can think of and use a battery of strategies for supporting learning

- recognises and uses new technologies in support of their own and their school students' learning.

3. Teachers as evaluators

A good teacher:

- takes time to assess and evaluate with others what they are doing and how they are learning

- can reflect, ponder and research into things.

Of course, there are also exceptional teachers, such as artists and poets who can create and distil for others what they have learnt for themselves, and those who welcome change and can initiate change as required.

Good teachers, however, need an equally good institutional framework within which to work and learn. In my Headteacher's Introduction to the Governors' Report in the Spring of 1995, I focused on Pam Sammons' eleven key factors for effective schools (Sammons et al., l994). Five of these move the school towards a learning institution and I outline below how these relate to the Hampstead context:

1. *Professional leadership from a leading professional which is firm and purposeful, with a participative approach.* One of the Ofsted inspection team said to me, 'You lead from the front'. I teach 25% of the week, until this year all examination groups. I enjoy learning to teach and to manage, and teaching to learn.

2. *Shared vision and goals showing unity of purpose, consistency of practice, collegiality and collaboration.* All staff are involved in establishing our constantly revised aim statement and joint policy development. Our Registered Inspector said: 'There is consistency of approach and policy across the whole school.'

3. *Concentration on teaching and learning.* We have established a curriculum entitlement policy and an academic code of conduct, as well as setting up entitlement for staff and school student work reviews. All embody our belief that everyone can learn and develop. To enable this to happen we have to exercise rigorous personal and professional standards.

4. *Purposeful teaching which exhibits efficient organisation, clarity of purpose, structured lessons and adaptive practice.* For the first year assignment for the Open University MA I am currently studying, I looked at Hampstead Year 8 school students' perceptions of good teaching. Their views validated the Sammons' factors on teaching, as well as amplifying them. These findings have been discussed and disseminated to school students, staff and governors and form the core of our academic code of conduct and our classroom observation checklist.

5. *A learning organisation.* This is the nub of it all. In a recent survey carried out by the staff development task group, 93% of the staff said they wanted to continue with further studies and research. Colleagues have been encouraged to take further qualifications, to undergo mentor training and to be actively involved with partner HE Institutions for initial teacher training. A proposal from a member of my senior executive team, that we top-slice our funding to create research and industry links, funds which colleagues can bid for, will be put in place from September l996. The same teacher, as part of her brief, has set up a staff training and resource library: I am busy filling it with videos of our own good practice. This means that even when colleagues get promotions and leave, there is a legacy of good practice captured on video for future use.

Initiatives like these are all part of our School Development Plan for 1995-8. It has been co-ordinated by one of my deputies, who has streamlined the final document so that it has become fully extended to every department and year team. It has also targeted the learning institution and one of the three main objectives: to develop the school as a learning community, the key action on this being:

- involve all teaching and support staff in 'Investors in People'

- establish a lesson observation programme in order to share good practice

- extend extra-curricular activities and monitor effect on achievement

- develop a community library, including an Independent Learning Centre

Related to this is an initiative developed with our vice-chair of governors. We have set up INSET on Socratic discussion to support Maths staff and link colleagues in HE. This exciting venture has opened our eyes to the power of structured conversations/dialogue to arrive at deep understandings of really complex problems such as the relationships between prime numbers. This has encouraged the Mathematics Department to pilot the cognitive thinking project with King's College, London in 1995/96 and we hope that increased improvements in numerical and linguistic achievement will result. It also provides further value for beginning teachers within this positive department.

I have found being part of a learning community exciting, particularly studying with the Open University. During the Autumn of 1993 I gained an OU Certificate in School Industry Links. From February 1994, I began an MA with a year module on Classroom Studies, carrying out a small research project on school students' perceptions of good teaching, and this has sharpened my own perceptions and made me more rigorous. In 1995, I studied developments in assessment and curriculum development. This year I finish with a module on education, training and employment. I intend to continue towards a doctorate, following in the footsteps of many of my colleagues and helping make the school a real learning community.

Being part of a learning community has other implications. Schools of tomorrow will need to prepare pupils to be effective world competitors, an exciting and challenging task, At a recent conference I set out ten things we have to do. They are:

- Be fearless, take risks and innovate

- Mobilise the intellectual, personal and social capabilities of all

- Have a mission, a strategy for achieving it and ambitious targets by which we can monitor success

- Develop learning communities

- Build on the strengths of all school students by taking their learning seriously

- Support school students' independent learning using peer counselling, work reviews, target setting and records of achievement

- Use all available technologies

- Develop education centres and community resources

- Ensure that core skills of literacy, numeracy, technology are sound

- Ensure progression, credit accumulation and transfer.

I have been giving this same message for a long time and much applies equally to how we should work with our beginning teachers. My job as Headteacher is to make all this a reality, by establishing the right climate and setting an example by focusing on my own learning about learning in the context of the school.

Staff development

Staff development has been a priority since industrial action ended at the end of the 1980s. Training targets are agreed with line managers to meet whole school aims and also as part of staff appraisal. Staff INSET with costings is formally set out as part of the School Development Plan. The school has always bid for significant money for training and with the introduction of LMS we continue to set aside time and money for both whole staff and individuals' training and development. Good use is also made of our own staff expertise. Staff appraisal follows the LEA procedures and is based on a successful staff development model. For many years we have had open testimonials, which teachers produce, submitting their own self-appraisal on an agreed pro-forma. Their head of department produces another appraisal on the same pro-forma, after seeing them teach. After a formal consultation a final testimonial is prepared. For the personal staff appraisal the only difference is the target setting, with costs written in to the School INSET Plan as part of the School Development Plan. In addition, portfolios are given to all staff to encourage further development (see fig. 2.2).

When we advertise for staff such as recently for a deputy headteacher, we always say we are looking for someone who is willing to continue their professional development. However, the opportunities for learning and for action research while training beginning teachers are only starting to be realised. We have always had good relations with our two nearest higher education providers – the Institute of Education, London and the University of North London, and have worked hard to bring down the barriers between us. (The following chapter and Chapters 11 and 12 explain these links in more detail.)

Fig. 2.2 PROFESSIONAL DEVELOPMENT FOLDER

CURRICULUM VITAE including pro-forma

CURRENT OPEN REFERENCE/SELF APPRAISAL

CURRENT TARGETS/AREAS FOR EXTENSION

FURTHER PROFESSIONAL STUDIES/COURSES/LINKS WITH HE
Diplomas, Certificates, MA, Doctorate

WHOLE SCHOOL INPUTS/EXTRA-CURRICULAR

PREVIOUS PROFESSIONAL EXPERIENCE

RELEVANT FAMILY/COMMUNITY EXPERIENCE

ACHIEVEMENTS RECORD
e.g. Certificates, letters of congratulation, commendation

INDUSTRY LINKS
eg Work Shadowing

MEMBERSHIP OF PROFESSIONAL ASSOCIATIONS
eg. NUT, ATL, NAS/UWT, SHA, ASE, BEMAS

CONTRIBUTIONS TO CURRICULUM DEVELOPMENT/WHOLE
SCHOOL POLICIES

PUBLICATIONS

PERSONAL ACTION PLANS

PERSONAL CAREER PLANS

With the Institute of Education in 1992, we were involved in the pilot for training articled teachers. Willing heads of department were given joint INSET to support their development as mentors – something they always acknowledged as valuable in their self-appraisal statements. One of my deputies contributed to the co-ordination of the whole project programme. She had also been allowed time off for a placement with the Department for Trade and Industry, and had a great deal to contribute. One of our experienced head of department mentors was appointed to be a lead HOD/advisory teacher for the LEA. This is an interesting model because it opened up her expertise to other Camden schools, enhanced her 'street cred' and kept her valued contributions to our school. She eventually took time to do her doctorate, which also fed back into the school, and is now running a PGCE course for languages teachers at the University of North London. (In Chapter 11, she describes the process of training mentors and provides more information on the background to her contributions.)

Both these models encouraged more reflective practice, had positive outcomes for staff development and gave professional support to beginning teachers. This was also facilitated by the strong teams that were being established at all levels within the school. The expertise generated by such activities can have important, if unforeseen, spin-offs. For example: I am a trustee of the Minerva Educational Trust, a charity dedicated to preparing young women for positions of leadership and responsibility. We raised over £10,000 to send an equal opportunities action pack for teachers to every school in Britain at the end of 1992. Each pack, which I edited, contained 18 photocopiable sheets, with suggestions, action plans and information which successful practitioners across the country found valuable in developing young people's confidence, skills and their commitment to play a more active role in public life. Although primarily targeted at girls, the practice was valid for all school students. A simple pro-forma was used for each trigger sheet, i.e. a one-paragraph rationale, followed by up to twelve action points and some relevant examples. There were sheets on topics such as girls into technology and computing, developing counselling skills, school student work reviews, setting up a school council, profiling and managing records of achievement. And all these were produced by colleagues at Hampstead School. Such public recognition of good practice is extremely important in strengthening the professional climate in the school.

Teachers as learners

We are all natural learners but to learn effectively, we need the conversations, the challenge and the opportunity to work with people and reflect on practice. It is something we all instinctively recognise in others and it is part of the reaching out and sharing, which is very hard to resist. Catalysts for change are vital in supporting teachers as learners and once the process has begun it cascades through an organisation. I first saw this in action at Abbey Wood School in south-east London, where we organised a whole staff residential conference on links with the community.

So we do not think of the training we give our beginning teachers and newly-qualified teachers (NQTs) as a training given only to them. We think of its value to the whole staff. At Hampstead we have also made it a policy to build in training by colleagues, so that it has become standard practice for colleagues to contribute to whole-school INSET and to cascade their own knowledge and expertise. Colleagues are also involved in whole school policy making, through our short term task groups, which give everyone opportunities to make a contribution. This would not be so positive were colleagues not already reflective and pro-active. (The level of professional talk among colleagues, who regularly stay until after six p.m. most days, is extremely high.) We believe in building strong teams to facilitate this learning and have spent time and money ensuring, for example, that departments have properly arranged working bases to facilitate their developing as strong teams who can support beginning and newly qualified teachers.

As a learning school, we have also shared with school students, beginning teachers and NQTs, our vulnerability and concerns over our own assignments and examination deadlines, so that they are aware that some of us too are studying. This has enhanced relationships and understanding and given us an empathy with each other that I did not expect. It seems to make it more likely that we get closer to Freire's 'authentic dialogue'. It has made me more aware of Bruner's view that successful mental sharings assure the passing on of ideas, given that 93 per cent of colleagues now wish to continue their own education. Stenhouse (1983) has said: 'If my words are inadequate look at the sketchbook of a good artist, a play in rehearsal, a jazz quartet working together' (p.195). That, I am arguing, is what good teaching is like. He goes on to suggest that we 'note, however, that the process of developing one's art as a teacher, or the art of teaching, which develops through individual artists – is a dialectic of idea and practice not to be separated from change'.

CHAPTER 3

MAKING IT WORK – THE SCHOOL-BASED TUTOR

Ruth Heilbronn

The Government expects that partner schools and higher education institution will exercise a joint responsibility for the planning and management of courses and the selection, training and assessment of school students. The balance of responsibilities will vary. (DFE, 1992, para. 14.)

It is important to understand the roles and responsibilities involved in building this partnership. This chapter describes the new and developing role of the school-based tutor in teacher training partnerships and how this differs from that of the subject-supervisor/mentor. The mentor role has recently been fully explored: both beginning teacher and school managers can be clear about what they should expect from those who are directly responsible for training subject teachers in school (see Chapters 9, 10 and 11). Books and learning packs on mentoring are appearing thick and fast and many contain useful and rigorous materials for those in the school who directly train beginning teachers. Clear guidance is available for teacher tutors, who are responsible for the induction of newly qualified teachers. Many LEAs have their own guidelines and monitoring procedures for newly qualified teachers (e.g. Earley, 1992; Earley and Kinder,1994; Ofsted, l993a). Current proposals for a national standard also pull together work of recent years to co-ordinate in-service training and staff development throughout a teaching career. The four key stages at which these standards are now defined are the newly qualified, the expert, the expert subject leader and the expert school leader stages (TTA, 1996).

Very little is available on the role of the school-based tutor/co-ordinator for the partnership programmes of initial teacher education. Yet certain guidelines need to be made explicit, so that the principles outlined in the DFE Circular above can be fulfilled. It is a developing role and one whose extent has not yet been mapped. (Unfortunately, even before its third birthday, the ideal of partnership arrangements has become strained, due to financial reasons.) The school-based tutor plays an essential role in pulling together the various aspects of the course for the beginning teachers, who may not even be aware of this liaison. To them partnership could seem to them like being pulled in more than one direction, as they work with ITET providers and school tutors at different times of their training. The school-based tutor needs to know and understand the details of all training arrangements, to ensure that the school provides the conditions to make them a reality. S/he also has a direct responsibility for the professional development of the beginning teachers in school.

School-based training in partnership with higher education is a new and developing provision. This account of how it is operated within our specific school training context illustrates how the role of the school-based tutor has developed over a two year period. Aspects of the new role of the school-based tutor emerge logically from the development of partnership and could, in fact, form a job description for the school-based tutor. I have deliberately avoided writing such a list: there are important elements which can be singled out but no one particular way of dividing this role and its responsibilities. In fact, the process of reflecting on how it is to be fulfilled, in a particular school and within specific partnership arrangements, has to be done afresh by each person who takes it on. The essential elements are outlined in the following inter-weaving of the history of partnerships as they are evolving at Hampstead School, with a description of the role of the school-based tutor.

'Excuse me. How to I get to partnership from here?'
'From here? If I were you I'd start from somewhere else'
There was a sense in which we did not choose our starting place for the new teacher training arrangements for 1994/95. It was legally required, with a statutory 60% school-based element, and we had to make it work. Our starting point was our pre-partnership arrangements, which were typical of other, similar schools at that time. In 1992/3, before the new courses, they covered a wide spectrum of different teacher training programmes, both post-graduate and B.Ed. Briefly they consisted of:

1. *An important link with the Institute of Education*, London, to develop an area-based teacher training scheme (described in more detail later, since it was the most formative programme for preparing the new role of the school-based tutor).

2. *Close liaison with the University of North London's Modern Languages Department* as it was developing its Modern Languages PGCE. Partnership evolved easily and naturally in this curriculum area, when the course leader was appointed to the university, from the LEA's advisory staff, having been a former Hampstead head of Languages. The wider development of this course is described in Chapter 11.

3. *Collaboration between the University of North London and the school Mathematics department.* The head and deputy head of the school Maths

department worked with the university department in the development of the B.Ed. course assessment. They then trained other subject supervisors, at both Hampstead and the University of North London (see Chapter 10).

The school also took beginning teachers from various higher education institutions, spread across different departments and varying over the years. Although some effective and long-standing relationships between curriculum departments at school and in HE were built up, this kind of *ad hoc* relationship mitigated against the evolution of partnership-type arrangements of the kind mentioned above. (For example, most recently we have had technology beginning teachers from the University of Middlesex's B.Ed course and Drama beginning teachers from the Central School of Speech and Drama, for whom we form a natural catchment area.)

This myriad of different arrangements was overseen by a member of the senior staff and administered on a day to day basis by the individual curriculum departments. No attempt was made to co-ordinate between departments (except for work within the area-based course, described later in this chapter and in Chapter 12), nor to spell out a common core of strategies or entitlements. Expectations of beginning teachers was different, even between different curriculum departments of the same higher education institution, which, as far as we could tell, no more communicated their aims and objectives to each other than we did. We did, of course ensure that subject supervisors were qualified and proficient. No more was required, nor expected at this stage.

Hampstead School and the London Institute of Education

In 1991/2, our LEA had been involved with a pilot scheme with the Institute of Education, London and had developed an area-based teacher training scheme which followed partnership principles, i.e. tutors from schools and the Institute of Education met regularly to shape the content and delivery of the PGCE course. Our school took an active role and the course ran for two years before the new school-based arrangements became statutory. The area-based link with the Institute of Education was made and maintained by a deputy head and involved overall co-ordination of the work of several subject departments, to ensure consistent expectations across departments. Moreover, a school tutor, working in conjunction with an Institute tutor, taught the professional studies elements of the course in school. In the other courses for which we took beginning teachers, professional studies had been entirely taught by the higher education providers in their institutions.

This school-based teaching gave the school tutor a new role in the training process and fruitful collaboration developed on issues surrounding our evolving practice. These developments, which foreshadowed the compulsory implementation of *partnership*, were productive for the school in several respects: providing recognition of our areas of expertise; developing the skills of the school-based tutor; establishing shared perceptions of the conjoint roles of school-based and institute tutor, and allowing the beginning teachers to receive precise and up-to-date practice-based illustrations of the issues in education under discussion. The joint tutorial session formed the basis of the current arrangements for the delivery of the professional studies elements of the Institute PGCE course.

The area based scheme was thus pioneering in its attempt to pull together different elements of teacher training and implement coherence and consistency, processes which were evaluated at the end of each year. Resultant changes were implemented yearly, to the overall benefit of the course. The school's experience in developing this course and collaborating with the LEA, with other schools and with the Institute of Education was significant in our subsequent training role.

When we previewed the changes to come from 1994/5 onwards we were committed to a partnership model like the one we had developed with the Institute of Education. We realised too that we had to formalise the Institute's way of working across all subject areas to ensure a coherent and consistent training experience. This was the first main task of the changed role of the school-based tutor.

The climate of the school was significant in this task. As other contributors to this book note also, we were already involved with our LEA in a model of appraisal based on the principle of staff development. School teacher appraisal was a nationally contentious issue in 1992/3 when we developed our school policy. We convened a group of teacher volunteers from across the school and they developed the school-specific aspects of our scheme and co-ordinated the first phase of its implementation. They issued guidelines to staff for producing teacher portfolios and encouraged all staff to evaluate and reflect on their practice.

The existence of this working group indicates a learning climate and shows that a collaborative structure was in place to create and disseminate new developments, which staff would be highly likely to accept. The process was clearly developmental: target setting and action planning were prominent. We were used to thinking that formative assessment promotes learning and that assessment criteria need to be made explicit. In both the assessment and marking policy which we were developing for school students and our procedures for the induction of newly qualified teachers, for example, development and learning were viewed in terms of negotiation, that is on the notions of shared aims and of dialogue. This went alongside our view of professional development as beginning at the initial teacher training stage, being consolidated in the newly qualified induction period and continuing to demand reflection and progression in subsequent stages of a teaching career. To help in this development, several subject supervisors had received additional training and support for their work as mentors of newly qualified teachers, run by the LEA, and the school had also been included in the study undertaken by the NFER into successful practices for induction of NQTs. This was a formative process for the school mentors who participated (see Earley and Kinder, 1994).

Implementing the national curriculum has made all schools focus on the essentials of curriculum planning and delivery. Ofsted has contributed to the new climate: preparing for an Ofsted inspection concentrates the school mind on development. Their manual has served as a focal point in outlining a model of good practice, even though the process of inspection itself may raise other issues. The Ofsted manual is clear about the criteria for successful teaching and learning and as a development tool is, despite controversy over the process of inspection, an influence for coherence in school development planning (Ofsted, 1993b).

From training group to code of practice

We formed a training group of teachers in the school, including everyone involved with teacher training and who would be taking on the newly expanded role of subject supervisor/mentor, and anyone else who expressed an interest. We met regularly throughout the spring and summer term of 1994 to clarify our aims and objectives for the new arrangements. As the senior management member involved with INSET, staff development, the induction of newly qualified teachers and teacher training, the role of school-based tutor became a development of my current job. Convening and co-ordinating a training group seemed to me the best way to develop a policy and ensure coherence and consistency of training across departments – which is crucial.

'If I were you I wouldn't start from here' goes the old joke, and indeed, the training group's early meetings revealed a confusion of paths, a patchwork of different tracks to QTS, across different institutions and departments. We had not debated the fundamentals of teacher training before and it was eye-opening to compare experiences across departments and institutions, noting the differences that existed in assessment, higher education institutes (HEIs), tutors, different departments within HEIs and mentoring support. We evolved a common core of concerns for the implementation of the new courses. We met together regularly and agreed on the principles which should underlie our commitment to training beginning teachers. We worked out the most essential aspects of their implementation, including basic management issues. And so developed a code of practice for beginning teachers on teaching placements in Hampstead School.

This code maintains that our school students are entitled to high quality teaching and beginning teachers to good training and teacher education. It declares class teachers as responsible for the classes taught and subject supervisors/mentors responsible for their beginning teachers. Beginning teachers' responsibilities are not specifically outlined in the code because as they are covered in the school's academic code of conduct, to which all teachers should conform. Setting out these entitlements clarified expectations and roles and made transparent the responsibilities. For example, there was no danger that 'student teachers' would be left to their own devices, while the class teacher took a rest in the staff room. The policy needs to be carefully monitored to prevent such things happening but once a climate of support and entitlement is built up, as at Hampstead, the responsibilities remain uppermost.

The code of practice was disseminated through school meetings before the new courses began in 1994/5. Disseminating basic information about the courses on a day to day basis, as well as about the wider concerns and issues, is another of my tasks. The role of communicator can mean raising the profile of teacher training to ensure commitment from parents and governors, which is how we began to plan for 1994/95. My work also involved keeping governors informed of our arrangements and doing the day to day negotiations on issues such as release and cover for mentor training.

As Appendix 2 on p.157 shows, the timetables of the classes taught by beginning teachers need co-ordination to ensure that there is an even spread of beginning teacher input. This prevents some classes having all the core subjects of the national curriculum taught by beginning teachers on teaching practice, which is unacceptable. Although most schools co-ordinated timetables in relation to this issue under pre-1995/6 arrangements, assuring consistency of mentoring support has been a new responsibility for me. Competence-based assessment is in place across all courses and monitoring the implementation of the Hampstead policy has become a key element of my work as a school-based tutor.

Monitoring requires holding meetings to exchange information on practice as well as on scheduling and checking that teaching files and the mentor logs are kept. The logs are an important formal reminder of the focus of a particular mentor session and the mentor's notes in them help the beginning teachers to set targets for their work between formal mentoring sessions. Also, should the beginning teacher feel that, for example, s/he had cause for complaint or grievance about support time, the log has recorded the work done together. Since mentor time at Hampstead school has been costed and given to the mentor as non-class contact time, having a log also enables the school to ensure that these sessions do take place. In practice, of course, far more time is given informally to the beginning teacher but having a log of the official sessions does at least provide a formal record.

Professional Studies

Partnership has let us provide training and development for beginning teachers in areas previously delivered in HE institutions. In all courses there is an *induction period* at the beginning of the teaching practice period, when the school-based tutor needs to put on a programme of introductory activities. (We have also produced a booklet for beginning teachers with our key policies, eg. for school student management, which cross-references to the staff handbook) These vary from course to course but most preliminary orientation activities include a tour of the school, a look at the school context and supporting statistics and some of the school policies; meeting senior staff; and tutorial support in researching an area-studies assignment, and providing a seminar to feed back the results of this assignment. In the Institute of Education course, the school functions within an area-based cluster, a group of three or four geographically close schools which collaborate on seminars for school-based professional work, so pooling resources and expertise. The area-based feedback is usually delivered in the cluster, and this enables us to visit other schools and host other tutors and beginning teachers at Hampstead.

Tracking school students also has to be arranged. All beginning teachers in their first practice spend one day shadowing a tutor group, one shadowing a school student with special educational needs and a third shadowing a bilingual school student requiring support with English. We consider these tracking activities extremely valuable, as this book will show. They are the beginning teachers' first glimpse of the range of pupils for whom they will ultimately be responsible. Tracking school students with particular needs focuses beginning teachers on issues with which they will have to grapple in their teaching practice, and feedback in seminars allows them to reflect on the challenges of differentiated teaching and the need to target individuals appropriately. The school tutor runs these seminars for oral feedback and discussion of issues raised by the tracking exercise and monitors the written reports of these shadows, which some of the courses require.

The teacher tutor also supervises all the pieces of work which will build into a final professional development portfolio, particularly on our Institute of Education course, where a variety of professional development activities (profiling tasks), form a focus for reflection on the aims and objectives of teaching and learning. The tasks require beginning teachers to write personal, analytic pieces on topics such as an audit of prior learning experiences, what kind of teacher they hope to be, observation of pupils whom they have tracked, reflections on their first teaching practice, and their targets for development, arrived at in discussion with their subject supervisor/mentor in the mentoring sessions and with the school-based tutor.

The profiling tasks also contain an element of school-based research (see Chapter 8). A staff library is maintained by the school tutor on funds earmarked from the PGCE budget. This is building into a valuable resource for all school researchers – particularly as staff are now donating their own texts and resources acquired during their own studies.

Stretching the budget: concerns and issues

As school-based tutor, I oversee the financial arrangements and negotiate timetable releases. Our greatest resource is our own staff, and to ensure that they have the time to support beginning teachers we have rationalised the practical management of the courses by setting up a teacher training budget cost-centre. We cost each period of mentor time, which we allocate to mentors as non-class contact time (by giving mentors supervision time as part of their teaching loading). Funding is monitored as it comes from HE and allocated to the staffing budget to cover mentor release. Some funding is top-sliced to give to departments for resources for the beginning teachers (photocopy cards, stationery etc.). Holding the funding centrally means that I can ensure it is targeted directly on teacher training. Departments earn 'extra funds', which they keep, if they host other HE initiatives, e.g. visiting teachers from abroad, but the 'training budget cost centre' is managed by the school-based tutor. This was arranged specifically in preparation for the implementation of Circular 9/92.

We enjoy partnership and we welcome the recognition of the expertise involved in largely practice-based teaching and learning. But the funding does not cover the time needed to do the job properly. Subject supervisors/mentors continue to be involved because of their own staff development and their commitment to training the next generation of teachers, but as more demands are made on their time we rely more and more on their dedication. The time we can actually allocate to them is not adequate for the job.

Even my hours as school-based tutor are inadequately funded. Not only does the role entail all the tasks described here but crises do occasionally arise that can take hours to sort out. These aspects of my pastoral role are insufficiently funded so the school-based coordinator has to juggle all the elements which turn promises in syllabuses into practice. Evidently many schools are finding this difficult. A recent report, based on a survey of three quarters of the partnerships between universities and schools in 1995/96 by a team funded by the Economic and Social Research Council, found that nearly a third of respondents reported difficulties in recruiting schools willing to take part in teacher training. (The report criticises the TTA's underestimation of the role of higher education in teacher training and concludes gloomily: 'the scope for many schools to move further towards the TTA model, let alone the SCITT (school centred initial teacher training) model in the foreseeable future seems decidedly limited' (Gardiner, 1996a).

We know the restraints on our HE partners and we are appreciative of the mentoring support and other facilities they offer us. Our concern is with central funding.

Conclusion

In terms of value for money then, we believe that we put far more time into the training process than is covered by the funding. Hampstead School staff also attend the HEIs to deliver seminars on professional issues and are on certain interviewing panels for prospective PGCE beginning teachers. They also receive prospective B.Ed. and PGCE candidates when possible and arrange a short induction programme to help them to prepare for their HEI interviews.

We enjoy these activities and endorse their value. Their funding does not nearly cover the time we give to them. Higher education has responded to our concerns by providing support in developing mentoring and tutoring skills. Some institutions and some curriculum departments have proved excellent. Others still need to do more for us. We look critically at the support given to us by institutions and evaluate their merits, since we too are under pressure to justify our resources, of which teacher time is by far the most expensive. For example, we took on an Open University PGCE beginning teacher in the Science department and then took another the following year because the support the Open University gave to them and to us was impressive. Their mentor training programme was well resourced with distance learning supporting material and offered a chance for the mentor to add a module to her MA.

We are increasingly looking at our ability to sustain the high quality teaching of beginning teachers within a supportive higher education context. What is required is on-going in-service training for everyone involved especially the subject supervisor/mentor and the school co-ordinator. Many teachers continue their own studies and access to HEI's library facilities should be granted automatically with partnership. Also needed is funding to cover the time for consultation meetings, both internally and with higher education. We are confident in our practical expertise. We reflect on what we do, research, record, evaluate in a wider context of education, and move on in our practice. What we often lack is detailed knowledge of relevant academic research which we all need to share and without which we will only offer a craft model of apprenticeship training.

We are overstretched and the problems remain – resources, time and funding. Yet it does seem to work and we enjoy it. The learning-school context embodied in the school's aims and to which the Head, governors and senior managers are all committed is fundamental to its success. The co-ordinator needs to be sufficiently senior in the school to be able to take an overview of developmental needs, in an ethos which values learning in its widest sense. But having this in place is not what makes the process work. It works only because of the subject supervisors/mentors. They are the lynch pin, as we shall see in subsequent chapters.

CHAPTER 4

ALL TEACHERS ARE SPECIAL NEEDS TEACHERS
Pat Mikhail

When they are first introduced to the school, our beginning teachers start to feel uneasy about their role as classroom teachers. They worry about whether they will be able to face a class, keep order, keep the students in their seats – let alone working. We try, at as early a stage as possible, to make the classroom situation real to them – all the courses in the partnership start with lesson observation. Tracking a pupil through one day is a particularly useful exercise, as many beginning teachers testify, especially when the BT tracks a school student with special educational needs (SEN) or with English as a second or additional language (EAL). Two of the beginning teachers' brief reports are given here in full. They provide good examples of the initial responses that many BTs have pupils with special educational needs. They also indicate beginning teachers' increasing awareness of the complex range of issues SEN involves, particularly when it also involves EAL needs. Both involved the tracking of Year 8 children, the first identified here as A and the second as S.

Observation of A. After a day shadowing A. I came home feeling completely drained and upset. She had spent over six hours in school and I couldn't honestly say that she's understood any more than 5% of the day.

The first lesson of the day was Design and the regular teacher was absent so the lesson was taught by a cover teacher. The aim of the lesson was to design a Swatch watch, using music as a theme. The first and most saddening fact was that A was sitting by herself at the end of a table of girls. When the girls were talking, A was half-heartedly listening but never actually spoke to any of them. Initially I found it hard to accept that she didn't have any friends: I thought that perhaps she was just at the bottom of the pecking order or that her friends were in a different group, not that in fact she was completely alone. While others in the lesson were laughing and joking, she sat quietly working, striving for perfection. I lost count of the number of times she drew the watch face with a compass and then rubbed it out because it wasn't quite right.

A was very reserved with the teacher, although this may have been due to the fact it was a cover teacher. When she was asking for help there was no real questioning, just the need for reassurance. Whilst the teacher was issuing instructions at the end of the lesson, everyone was talking and A looked as if she was listening. However, from the vacant look on her face, her thoughts were elsewhere.

The second period was Maths, and I spent it with A and a classmate in the library, doing some work on angles and the use of a protractor. The main concepts had been introduced in the previous lesson but I had to repeat every fact before the task could even be attempted. A had problems accepting that the total number of degrees in a triangle add up to 180. Her classmate behaved very differently, for he could remember that there are 180 degrees in a triangle but flew into a panic when he made an error or guessed incorrectly. A was beginning to open up a bit more. Both children displayed coordination problems in using the protractor. I was unsure whether it was because it was an unfamiliar piece of equipment or a genuine coordination problem.

I felt it would have been unfair to shadow A during break time, even though I was intrigued as to whether she had any friends. At the beginning of period 3, I was greeted with an enormous grin from A. The science lesson was very positive, with constructive and encouraging advice for everyone from the Head, who is a science teacher. The aim of the lesson was to investigate the effects of exercise on breathing. Again A sat alone, quiet and withdrawn, but kept looking at me to see if I was watching her. The teacher was giving instructions about what the pupils should write about in terms of aim, hypothesis, prediction, report, results and how it all should be presented. A did not understand any of it. She was not really paying attention. Several times I looked over and she was scribbling on her book, counting bonus points and at one point doing a quick sketch of someone vaguely resembling me! A was in a different world: she stared vacantly at the blackboard and copied exactly what was written before her, even to the extent that where the teacher had ringed an important word, A also duly ringed the same word in her book, not knowing what the word meant or why it was ringed.

As the lesson progressed, the class was divided into mixed pairs in order that someone could use the stopwatch to record the number of breaths in a minute. A even showed signs of confusion at this simple task and I'm unsure whether she counted her breaths correctly. There was some reluctance to communicate with her partner and she shifted uneasily in her seat while he was talking to her. I found this situation very distressing, as this was an ideal opportunity for a friendship to be forged, but to no avail. A was just as quiet and reserved.

Period 4 was Art. The class were all very high and yet again A was vacant, sad and alone. The lesson was a development on the work done previously. In the last lesson, they had worked on their skin tones, producing a colour chart of their own skin tones. Today's lesson was to start painting a self-portrait. It took A at least thirty minutes to draw a shape that resembled her face and the rest of the lesson was spent in a confused state, because she could not remember how she made the correct skin colour last lesson. Again, there was little student-student interaction and only a small amount of student-teacher interaction. This was typical of what had been displayed all day, i.e. vacant gazes and the need for reassurance very similar to behaviour displayed by children at Key Stage 1 and 2.

Overall, I was saddened to see the isolation of this young girl: she was permanently alone, dazed and confused. There are two main schools of thought in terms of educating children with SEN. One is through withdrawal, i.e. she would have special lessons and rarely interact with other, more able students. This could lead to further isolation and a feeling of worthlessness because she was having special lessons but, bearing in mind the lack of student interaction, perhaps more withdrawal lessons could be used. Currently A is only withdrawn from English lessons because it is her second language, but she really is having difficulty coping with the other lessons and I don't feel it is because of a language problem. Since observing A and reading the school's curriculum support booklet I have discovered that A is currently awaiting assessment.

2. Observation of S. All three classes were of about twenty students. In Science, S was given special support from a 'support teacher'. He has this extra help for four periods in the week. Today S was generally quiet, although apparently this is not always the case. My first impression of S in the classroom was of a student who is particularly self-involved and values having individual teacher attention. He was not disciplined in any of the three lessons, hardly engaging with the other students at all apart from R, who has Down's Syndrome. In English they sat next to each other and spent a fair amount of time talking. S has a limited concentration span and is unable to keep up with the pace and level of the work in the class. His method of coping with this situation is to cut off. He is easily distracted by details around him – his pens, shirt buttons, bag etc., or he spends a lot of time doodling and drawing in his book with his head down. As I spent time with him I began to feel his isolation. Activity is all around him but he is not part of it.

In the science class with the support teacher, he was forced into connection with the general activity. He was made to order his work and engage with the problems and tasks at hand. His pace was much slower than the rest of the class, however, but with this guidance he was able at least to be a part of the class. In the other periods where he had no special attention the task of involving him fell to the teacher. With twenty students to work with, the teacher is constantly juggling with time and the sporadic attention he received, I felt, was insufficient.

S needs constant support to be able to engage at the moment. He knows without this input he is lost and his time is wasted. The issue, I think, is how needy is S? Would he be better engaged in a specific class out of mainstream education? Or is it more beneficial to him to remain in the normal school life with the limited support he currently receives? It seems so much of his time and his own self is lost. Maybe he realises more and more how far behind his peers he is. Does this continuously compound his isolation? With limited funding there is very little that can be done.

This was a very sad experience.

The issues raised in these two accounts are reasonably common in Hampstead School and in most other urban secondary schools. They demonstrate the complexity of the learning needs which just one student in a class can present. The tracking exercise increases awareness and raises the question as to how we may best support beginning teachers to deal effectively with such children. At Hampstead School this role is undertaken mainly by the Curriculum Support [CS] Department. It consists of the equivalent of nine full-time teachers, three secondary helpers (assistants) and three part-time volunteers and is based in three rooms in the new block at Hampstead. We are centrally positioned in the school, which provides ample opportunity for teachers, beginning teachers, parents and students to drop in for help and assistance.

We try to operate an open-door policy and BTs are welcome to come in for help and to make use of the department's resources before, during and after school. We do not feel our support of students begins and ends in the lessons. In our room we try to create a secure place for students and we hope that through this policy we can deal with minor problems before they become major. A quotation from a Year 10 student who has succeeded beyond all expectations, sums up our philosophy:

> The Curriculum Support room is good. I go in when I have a problem like if I'm upset or sick. I also go in for help with homework. I like calling in because it is warm and to say hello. Sometimes I'm just being nosy!

To broaden the context for the tracking exercises we follow with a session outlining the guidelines we follow, going back to the Warnock Report on Special Education (DES 1978), which stated that all pupils should be educated following common goals and with common purposes. Building on this report the 1988 Education Act recommended entitlement to a common curriculum. (For a full discussion on this background see Capel, Leask and Turner, 1996, pp 199- 212). *The Code of Practice on the Identification and Assessment of SEN* (DFE, 1994b) was introduced in the 1993 Education Act. This states that a child has a learning difficulty if he or she:

a) has a significantly greater difficulty in learning than the majority of children of the same age;

b) has a disability which either prevents or hinders the child from making use of educational facilities of a kind provided for children of the same age in schools within the area of the local education authority;

c) is under five and falls within the definition at (a) or (b) above or would do if special educational provision was not made for the child. (DFE, 1994b, p.5)

In addition the Code of Practice states that a child must not be regarded as having a learning difficulty solely because the language or form of language of the home is different from the language in which he or she is or will be taught.

We aim to identify the additional needs of all learners as soon as possible and to provide for these needs, within the acknowledged limitations on resources, with minimal exemption from the National Curriculum. For this reason we take care to ensure that beginning teachers training with us are fully briefed on special needs early in their course. When they see the situation from the point of view of the learner, after having shadowed individuals or groups, it may still come as a surprise that most of the time, the children's needs have to be met in the ordinary classroom. We try to instil an understanding of the school's expectation that all teachers must be alert to a child's individual needs and that class planning for differentiated learning is therefore essential. This alerts beginning teachers to the need to differentiate their teaching to match individual school students, a skill which they, like all teachers, work on throughout their time with us on teaching practice. Because our children have needs in all curriculum areas, we believe strongly that all teachers are special needs teachers. We believe also that all children have the right to individual attention in some form or other.

To help in all this we provide in-service training to our newly qualified teachers, to ensure that they have as wide a range of information and support as possible from the Curriculum Support Department. In addition, there is a series of on-going activities to support both staff and beginning teachers. Some of the main elements of this support are:

• Verbal day-to-day contact plus staff briefing-sessions every Monday morning

• Background information booklet given to all staff in September

- Notes on pupils' special needs made by all teachers on a class recording sheet and help given by department in planning differentiation objectives

- Meetings organised by CS Department, focusing on a tutor group or individual pupil

- Individual Education Plans (IEP) circulated to subject teachers, tutors, Heads of Year (HOY) and the parents concerned.

The passing of information has to be a two-way process and this is often difficult in a school of our size. However, with the pastoral role of all teachers so prominent in the school, we do find the time. We also try to have CS Department teachers as tutors in each pastoral year to support the year teams.

Clearly, then, the school regards all teachers as special needs teachers. The CS Department advocates and helps to develop a range of teaching methods to deal with a wide range of learning difficulties and sees it as important that this knowledge is shared with the beginning teachers, as well as with the staff more generally. What does this mean in practice and how do we present this aspect of our work to the beginning teachers? We comment on the lesson observations they have made in the first week's tracking exercise. We ensure that they understand that at some point in their school career many pupils may have particular needs which may prevent them from gaining maximum access to the curriculum, to extra-curricular activities and to other resources and facilities. We inform the beginning teachers of the Code of Practice Stages discussed below and that children may experience several kinds of difficulties impeding their learning.

The teaching methods are similar to those found in most secondary schools and are identified to beginning teachers early on. Amongst the most important are:

- Mainstream classroom, with differentiated work making materials/ programmes accessible to all

- Mainstream classroom with small group teaching; subject teacher providing additional help while the rest of the group get on with work

- Partnership/team-teaching: support teacher sharing responsibilities

- Mainstream classroom with support teacher working alongside learners in the classroom to help those targeted as having SEN. Support may vary from week to week: in class all lesson, withdrawal for part, subject teacher removing some from the class, etc

- Mainstream classroom with individual support teacher (IST) working alongside specific statemented learners. Can help others but primarily responsible for one child; support can vary as above

- Withdrawal of students to work individually or in small groups out of the classroom on a specific identified topic.

- Regular weekly individual/group withdrawal on literacy/numeracy.

Ideally, BTs observe and are involved in many of these activities. In addition the CS Department aims to work with beginning teachers to promote common aims, support good order and encourage a good working environment. It gives specific advice in relation to resources, differentiation of worksheets and more general lesson strategies.

In practice it is sometimes difficult for a beginning teacher to grasp the implications of all this for their teaching. Although the levels that some of our children are working at can cause difficulties for them as a class teacher, the BTs can understand the sheer enjoyment we get in our department, as the following examples show:

- The transformation of a Year 7 boy who spent a number of hours, when he first joined Hampstead, talking to the special educational needs co-ordinator (SENCO) in the boys' toilets from behind a locked door. He had acute difficulties with literacy and with his own self-estem. Two years later, he is now reading a part in *Romeo and Juliet* in front of his class.

- The student who at his primary school was out of his lessons because of behavioural difficulties. When he arrived at Hampstead he could not read the word 'a'. Now in Year 8, during a recent lesson he was heard to say with great pride, 'I'm reading!"

- The girl who had to be escorted around school in Year 7, who would not converse, and who was at one stage considered to be more suited to a special school. Now she initiates conversations, is confident and successfully going out of school on work experience.

These examples also emphasise the individual differences and the range of abilities beginning teachers need to cater for when planning their lessons and also how important it is, when taking over a class, to talk to the teacher and find out about the children in class. The Curriculum Support department sees itself as a further resource to advise and support beginning teachers in this.

Information for Staff

At any one time the Warnock Report of 1978 estimated that nationally, approximately 20% of the school population have special educational needs. (DES, 1978). It is reasonable to assume that this will be higher in certain schools, namely inner-city comprehensives such as ours. Since it is all teachers' responsibility to provide for students' needs, balancing the needs of the individual with the needs of the whole school, the CS department aims to support all the teachers in the school in this task. What follows is an outline of the information we give our staff to develop and monitor their awareness of the issue. This information can also be used as reference material by beginning teachers. Although it is in general applicable to most other schools of similar nature, some is specific to the school and is noted as such.

The 1993 Education Act: The 1993 Education Act has 6 parts, section 3 being 'Children with Special Needs'. Its ideas have built upon and largely replaced the 1981 Act and were geared to raising the quality of provision for all SEN students. It required the Secretary of State to issue a Code of Practice giving practical guidance to LEAs and governing bodies of all maintained schools on their responsibilities towards children with SEN. It recommends that schools should identify children's needs and take action to meet those needs as early as possible. A staged approach is suggested, starting with the subject teacher. Subsequent stages increasingly involve other teachers and outside agencies in a process which may culminate in a formal assessment and a Statement of Special Educational Needs.

At Hampstead we operate a five stage Model of Assessment and Provision, but in certain cases we are able to jump stages:

Stage 1: Class or subject teachers identify or register a student's special educational needs and take appropriate action (possibly in consultation with CS department). Differentiating the lessons is the main tool. If more help is needed a 'Cause for Concern' form is filled in for the CS Department.

Stage 2: The school's SEN co-ordinator (SENCO) takes lead responsibility for gathering information and for co-ordinating the student's special educational provision, working with the student's teachers. At this stage the first Individual Education Plan (IEP) will be drawn up to help ensure a consistent approach by subject teachers and to raise awareness of abilities, problems and expectations and ongoing specialised work. A review is arranged and if it is seen that more help is needed, the student may pass on to Stage 3.

Stage 3: Teachers and the SENCO are supported by specialists from outside the school (see list of support agencies below). If a student is still not making satisfactory progress, after consultation with parents, the educational psychologist is approached and the student may move to Stage 4.

Stage 4: The LEA considers the need for a statutory assessment and if appropriate, makes a multi-disciplinary assessment which leads to Stage 5.

Stage 5: The LEA panel considers the need for a formal and official statement for special educational needs and, if appropriate, draws up such a statement and arranges, monitors and reviews provision. Within the official Statement for Special Educational Needs, Part 2 of the statement describes the child's special educational needs and Part 3 outlines what the school should be providing, usually including a time-allocation funded by the LEA.

It is a requirement that each child's Statement is reviewed annually by a panel. Those on the panel include a representative of the education authority, the school's educational psychologist, the SENCO, the deputy head of Hampstead responsible for Special Needs, the student's individual support teacher, closely involved teachers, the school nurse and doctor, parents and any other involved outside support agencies. The recommendations of these meetings are passed to the LEA. This involves a heavy meeting commitment in November and December for the school.

The important wording in the Code of Practice is 'have regard'. It is accepted that the implementation of the code will develop over time and will vary according to the size, organisation, location and number of students in the school. It is recognised that there is a continuum of need to be reflected in a continuum of provision. We have implemented the code as a 'rolling programme' initially working with Year 7 and now, in its second year, working with Years 7 and 8.

It was mentioned earlier that there was a range of outside agencies which support the school in these matters and can be involved in the various stages of the code. These include:

The Educational Psychologist. The educational psychologist who visits the school regularly has been assigned to us by the LEA and her time in school is planned by the head of Curriculum Support. While statutory work (i.e. stages 4 and 5) has to take priority, the educational psychologist is also involved with students at Stage 3 (assessing children's needs and advising on interventions) and at Stage 2 (discussing students and/or strategies with teachers). As well as working with individual students, she works on more general SEN issues such as implementing the SEN code of practice, strategies for addressing behavioural or learning difficulties, use of assessment techniques, and the assessment of bilingual and refugee students. She also contributes to departmental and whole-school INSET and to other meetings in school. All referrals to the educational psychologist are made through the Curriculum Support department, including requests for special considerations in GCSE/A Level examinations.

The Educational Social Worker. The statutory role of the educational social worker [ESW] concerns attendance, SEN, exclusions and child protection. With an allocation of two days a week to Hampstead, there are weekly appointments with the deputy head and year heads and discussions with the head of SEN. The educational social worker has a monitoring and advisory role in SEN stages 2 and 3 and where appropriate, the ES contributes to the full assessment advice in stage 4. Children can be seen by the ES for counselling in school in addition to home visits if required.

The School Medical Service. The school nurse's role primarily involves health surveillance. All new admissions, for example, have an initial medical check, health interviews take place in Year 9 and there is an on-going school-wide immunisation programme. The school nurse has a liaison and advisory role with teachers and outside agencies and works closely with heads of year and the Curriculum Support department when there is a medical concern. She helps provide the medical report which is required in the interdisciplinary assessment procedure (stage 4) and she also attends case conferences and annual reviews (stage 5) when appropriate.

Peripatetic teachers. There are a number of children in Hampstead who have sensory impairments. These are visited by peripatetic teachers for the visually impaired, the hearing-impaired and sometimes an occupational therapist. The Curriculum Support department organises these visits and supervises the use of any appropriate equipment provided by such bodies as Cenmac (The Centre for Micro-Assisted Communication).

Careers Service. The school has a mainstream careers officer who regularly visits Hampstead, working closely with our careers and industry links teacher. The careers officer has access to specialist special needs officers who can give information on special college courses and training programmes as well as on new legislation. At Hampstead, the careers officer works primarily with Year 10 upwards, when students have group sessions on general career areas as well as individual interviews. Children with special needs are targeted for early interviews and have the option of further individual interviews if necessary. The careers officer is invited to all transitional annual reviews of statemented students aged 14 or over and at stage 5 and any subsequent reviews.

Tavistock Clinic. Hampstead School is fortunate to be close to this world-famous clinic. Young people suffering from trauma of various kinds may be referred to it and if accepted for treatment, therapists at the clinic work individually with the young person. In some cases it is recommended that therapy is conducted together with other family members. Sessions are usually an hour long, once a month.

Refugee co-ordinator. A teacher has been appointed to take special responsibility for this group of students and this is fully discussed in Chapter 7.

The department can give guidance on some of the other important issues that beginning teachers often raise. Some of the most frequent are:

1. What procedures are in place to ensure a smooth transfer between primary and secondary school? During the spring term, when secondary school places have been allocated, staff from Hampstead's Curriculum Support department and the Head of Year 7 visit the feeder primary schools and interview both students who will be moving to Hampstead and their teachers. Primary transfer profiles are compiled and student additional needs (PAN) forms are completed. Information is exchanged between Hampstead and the feeder schools, e.g. Individual Education Plans (IEPs) are passed on. A letter is sent to families about arrangements for the parents' evening and induction day during the summer term. In addition all the new students and their parents are interviewed during the summer term. This is where the school's official partnership with parents begins, which involves parents in supporting their children at school. Parents are invited to meet the head of year and tutors at a new parents' evening, while students are invited for the new students' induction day, at which they meet the head of year and their new tutor group and experience some 'taster' lessons.

School staff meet at this point to produce balanced tutor groups which reflect the achievement, gender and ethnic diversity of students entering the school. In addition, pupils in primary schools with statements of special needs should have their statement reviewed before they transfer to secondary school.

2. How does the school ensure that the transfer between primary and secondary school of information about a student's educational needs is a smooth one? Do all teachers understand the process and does it inform their teaching of Year 7? On entry, all students in Year 7 are given the London Reading Test. Those students with low scores may have difficulty coping with the curriculum and further testing may be needed. In addition, meetings discuss tutor groups and individual students. This is also a time when individual education plans (IEPs) can be drawn up. IEPs are reviewed twice yearly, unless it is felt a shorter time is required.

3. How are students screened who are taken on roll other than at primary transfer? Bilingual Support and Curriculum Support (CS) departments work together with the relevant head of year, in relation to this group of students. There is an initial interview with parents and students, followed by screening tests and orientation. This programme is timetabled into one morning a week.

4. How do teachers alert the CS Department to any concerns? Where a subject teacher or a beginning teacher feels a student has an additional need, they may discuss it with a CS teacher. Then a 'cause for concern' form is completed, in line with the directives on good practice set out in the Code of Practice (DFE, 1994b). Students may refer themselves if they feel in need of additional help. Parents may also contact us to discuss their concerns.

5. What strategies could be useful for a beginning teacher when responding to behavioural and social concerns? The school expects that all students work intellectually, practically and socially to the best of their ability. Positive acclaim and accreditation are used as rewards: sanctions and counselling are applied when necessary for under-achievement and anti-social behaviour. As teachers managing behaviour in class, beginning teachers need to create an environment within which an individual can learn and the teacher can work effectively. If the teacher spends an inappropriate time on one student, others may have difficulty working effectively. In addition, beginning teachers at this stage need to be aware of maturation issues. Sometimes beginning teachers see children as rebellious when in fact insufficient guidance has been given to the students about boundaries and structures.

We attempt to show BTs that it is possible to change inappropriate behaviour given the right encouragement and positive reinforcement. Strategies could include avoiding labelling the student as disruptive and referring to disruptive incidents instead; recognising that disruptive incidents are often the result of insecurity and low self-esteem; attempting to identify what triggers off the negative behaviour in order to avoid the situation recurring.

In conclusion, our work with beginning teachers is similar to our work with all staff in the school and shows that students who have special needs are the concerns of all teachers in the school. It is vital that responsibility for educating the whole range of learners is seen as fundamental to each teacher's role. All teachers can confidently assert that they are good special needs teachers when they are informed, supported and capable of dealing with the issues involved.

CHAPTER 5

IT: EVERY TEACHERS' SECOND SUBJECT?
Phil Taylor

In recent years, teachers have had to get used to a new responsibility – they are now expected to teach information technology skills. All ITET require beginning teachers to develop IT capability. We introduce our beginning teachers to IT early in their induction period. During their time on teaching practice they frequently return to the IT co-ordinator to develop their own skills, to learn how to use IT in the classroom and, in some cases, to carry out tasks.

Beginning teachers and IT requirements
At Hampstead we develop an understanding of IT requirements largely in a cross-curricular context. The information which is given to beginning teachers in their introductory IT session is built upon throughout their teaching practice. They need first to understand that all teachers are now expected to able to teach IT skills. Any possible doubts about this expectation have been laid to rest by the revised National Curriculum. It is a statutory requirement that school students should be given opportunities, where appropriate, to develop and apply their IT capability in their study of National Curriculum subjects. This applies to all National Curriculum subjects except PE (although there are some good opportunities for learning IT skills within PE as well).

Several models for the delivery of IT capability have emerged. In secondary schools, where subject-based teaching prevails, IT capability is either taught as a subject in its own right, or developed within other subjects. It is clear that schools following the former approach alone will not be meeting their statutory obligations. So in practice, most schools either follow the latter approach or a combination of the two.

Many teachers argue that school students need to be taught some IT skills in isolation before they can usefully apply them within their other subjects. This also helps to ensure that a basic IT entitlement for all school students is established. The disadvantage of this approach is that both IT resources and the IT co-ordinator's time are preoccupied by 'IT lessons'. Few schools are sufficiently well-resourced or staffed with IT specialists to prevent separate IT lessons and cross-curricular IT work detracting from each other. This is magnified when the school offers GCSE, GNVQ or A-Level options in information technology, information systems, computer science or computing. Such courses allow a few school students who are interested in IT to further their knowledge and skills but this is inevitably at the expense of the rest, who have less access to IT resources and the IT specialists' time.

Other schools, like Hampstead School, have chosen to remove IT entirely from the timetabled curriculum, easing resources and the IT co-ordinator's time, to enable IT capability to be integrated across the curriculum. This is a bold approach. To ensure entitlement, all teachers need to be prepared to develop their own IT skills and provide opportunities for school students to develop theirs. Of course, the IT co-ordinator can offer INSET for teachers and is also available to support them in the classroom. Another important issue is assessment – it is difficult to build an adequate picture of each student's IT capability when the requisite skills are being taught across the curriculum. Also, there are no IT courses for those school students who wish to develop more specialist IT skills and acquire formal IT qualifications. However, some IT syllabuses now take cross-curricular activity into account, or internal systems of certification for IT capability can be set up.

Nevertheless, it is important that opportunities are provided for progression to more advanced IT skills. Underpinning the cross-curricular approach is the belief that the curriculum itself can supply the best contexts in which to learn IT skills as well as apply them. This works only if teachers are willing to get involved and if the IT co-ordinator and other IT specialists, including beginning teachers, can support them.

There is another important issue relating to the teaching of IT capability across the curriculum – enhancement. Quite rightly, beginning teachers, like teachers more generally, are only willing to integrate IT into their subject teaching if it brings about a perceived learning enhancement. There is a great danger that if school students are learning IT skills for the first time the IT can get in the way of the subject teaching. IT capability is acquired in a useful context, while subject-based learning is motivated and reinforced by the use of IT. It is the IT co-ordinator's role to help bring about a shift from IT interference to IT enhancement, so that IT skills and subject-based skills or concepts are mutually improved.

Some IT co-ordinators express the fear, probably with tongue in cheek, that if they are successful in their task of integrating IT into the curriculum they will eventually do themselves out of a job! This is highly unlikely, as the field of IT is changing all the time and new teachers continue to enter schools with different IT experiences. There is never any room for complacency – a school simply cannot say that 'IT is well integrated into the curriculum' and leave it at that. To keep IT integrated, work is required: developing new opportunities for using IT, exploring new technologies, furthering the skills of new and existing teachers. It is to be expected that, if ITET programmes are working properly, new teachers will enter the profession with ever-better IT skills. However, many new teachers with well-developed IT skills of their own, still start their first job having had little experience of using IT in the classroom with school students. The reasons for this are complex but some of those relating to school practice deserve further examination.

The practical realities of schools often dictate that IT cannot be used in the most 'natural' ways. For example, the drafting and re-drafting afforded by word processors when producing written work is a great advantage. Most writers using word processors will enter their ideas directly into the machine, then re-work them over time. With limited access to resources, without their own personal computer, it is difficult for school students to work in this way. School students often end up 'typing up' work that they have already produced and edited on paper. However, short pieces such as poems can easily be created and edited on a word processor in a single lesson. Another possibility is to give school students a piece of text to work on, perhaps something written with a particular bias that needs editing to make it more neutral. In schools, where circumstances are often less than ideal, it is perhaps better to use IT in ways that take maximum advantage of its power as a tool. However, teachers need to be trained in these techniques.

IT capability

The use of a word processor to draft and re-draft ideas in the written form is certainly an example of IT capability. At this stage, it is useful to look more closely at what IT capability actually means. The National Curriculum states that:

> Information technology (IT) capability is characterised by an ability to use effectively IT tools and information sources to analyse, process and present information, and to model, measure and control external events. This involves: using information sources and IT tools to solve problems; using IT tools and information sources, such as computer systems and software packages, to support learning in a variety of contexts; understanding the implications of IT for working life and society (DFE, 1995).

It should be noted that, although predominantly concerned with the use of computer hardware and software, IT can extend to other areas such as audio, video and music technologies. To examine IT capability in more detail, it can be divided into five strands, summarised below:

- *Communicating Information* The use of IT to communicate ideas in different contexts, taking audiences into account. Different forms of information, such as text, graphics, sounds, animation and video, should be presented and integrated as appropriate

- *Handling Information* The use of IT to store, process and analyse qualitative and quantitative information. The use of different information sources to select and display information, questioning its plausibility

- *Modelling* The use of IT-based models and simulations to explore real and imaginary situations, predicting outcomes and identifying patterns and relationships. The use of IT to create models

- *Measurement and Control* The use of IT to collect data from sensors and the use of IT to control devices and events

- *Applications and Effects* The review of IT experiences, examining the advantages and disadvantages, relating them to wider applications. Discussion of the social, economic and moral issues relating to IT.

The skills and activities that make up IT capability are most commonly taught via the use of generic, or general-purpose software, such as word processors, graphics programs, databases, spreadsheets and so on. Generic programs have little or no subject matter or content contained within them – they are content-free. They are essentially tools for carrying out and facilitating tasks, like text production and data handling. Such programs are often described as emancipa-tory, as they can free the user from otherwise tedious and time-consuming work. Generic software programs, however despite being content-free, usually impose certain restraints on the user in the range of features they provide and the mode of operation they demand.

In addition, schools often make use of specific software. Recent forms of these include reference tools such as CD-ROMs and integrated learning systems (ILS). This type of software differs from generic software, in that it is content-carrying. With generic software, it is the user that generates the content; with specific software, the content is built into its design. Specific software attempts to teach concepts or skills by presenting them in various ways and involving school students in activities. Some of these activities may contribute to IT capability, but many will not. For example, using an information source (perhaps a CD-ROM) to carry out some historical research, or exploring a simulation of a scientific process are both clearly identified as elements of IT capability. On the other hand, carrying out a computer-based question and answer exercise, however valuable as a learning aid, is not.

Although generic and specific are two distinct types of software, there are relationships between them. It is possible to combine the use of each type, for example by finding useful information from a CD-ROM, and then re-working it for a presentation using a desktop publishing or graphics program. There are other situations where generic software can be used for specific purposes. For example a computer model of a situation or process can be set up by a teacher, using a spreadsheet, for school students to explore. The teacher creates the model using a generic program, but for the school students the content is already defined.

Fig. 5.1.

GENERIC SOFTWARE –
general-purpose, tools, content-free

• **Word processing and DTP**
For producing documents, essays, reports, presentations

• **Graphics packages**
For painting, drawing, illustrating, designing, presenting

• **Databases and spreadsheets**
For handling data, charting, modelling, analysing, predicting

• **Modelling tools**
For creating models of situations or processes

• **Authoring programs**
For creating multimedia presentations and applications

• **Programming languages**
For creating computer applications

• **Measurement and control programs**
For collecting data from sensors and controlling external devices

• **Other tools**
For making music, accounting, organisers etc.

SPECIFIC SOFTWARE –
subject-related, content-carrying

• **Practice and exercise programs**
For question and answer, trial and error, challenges, text manipulation and reconstruction, simple games

• **Closed simulations and decision-making programs**
For simulating situations or processes, learner makes decisions (changes variables) which alter the outcome, 'closed' – limited outcomes

• **Open simulations and exploratory environments**
For exploring situations or processes, learner can control 'rules' of the situation, 'open' – unlimited outcomes, 'Microworlds'

• **Integrated learning systems (ILS)**
Complete systems, wide range of skills and concepts taught, mainly 'instructional' but becoming more interactive, diagnostic, individualised to school student's needs, can produce reports of school student progress

• **Reference tools (CD-ROMs, large databases, World Wide Web)**
Resources for browsing and extracting information, often multimedia – text, pictures, sounds, animations and video

The different types of generic and specific software currently available are outlined below. The classifications are intended as general guidelines – some programs fall into more than one category.

Applications and learning environments

One of the greatest benefits afforded by such a wide range of available software is the variety of different learning environments that can be supported. The type of software used and the way in which it is used, greatly affect the learning environment. There are opportunities for many different teaching/learning styles, such as: private study, group work, problem-solving and decision making, role play, tests and challenges, investigative work and fact-finding.

Different computer programs offer the user different levels of control and users will have their own perception of, and way of dealing with, this control. At one extreme, the computer is completely in control, for example, a demonstration program. At the other extreme, the user is in total control of the computer, for example, when programming. Most programs lie somewhere between these two extremes and judging the balance of control evaluates their potential for learning. This balance of control between the computer and the user will vary along a continuum, according to the type of activity for which the computer program is designed. Some programs promote several different activities and could therefore occupy more than one position on a continuum. For example, a simulation program may include demonstrations and also investigations. Similarly, reference tools can be used for general browsing, more structured inquiries, or extracts may be taken for inclusion in a presentation.

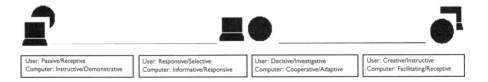

User: Passive/Receptive Computer: Instructive/Demonstrative	User: Responsive/Selective Computer: Informative/Responsive	User: Decisive/Investigative Computer: Cooperative/Adaptive	User: Creative/Instructive Computer: Facilitating/Receptive

Although much of the balance of control is built into the design of a computer program, the experience and characteristics of the user may also be significant. A positive approach to the software, together with guidance from a teacher, can lead to shifts along the continuum towards more user-controlled activities. The context in which a program is being used will also affect the balance of control. For example, a graphics program can be used in a completely open-ended way, as a tool for creative expression. Alternatively, the teacher could use the same program to give the school students a particular design or pattern to edit, perhaps by trying out different colour-schemes.

It might be useful to consider where the following IT activities would appear on the continuum above, and also to what extent they contribute to a student's IT capability:

- Browsing a hypermedia CD-ROM with basic navigation tools and 'hotwords'

- Playing an arcade type game ('shoot 'em up')

- Creating a newsletter using a DTP or word processing program

- Using a practice and exercise program to answer questions set by the computer program

- Using a spreadsheet to model a situation or process

- Searching a large database or CD-ROM using search statements

- Using a sensor connected to the computer to collect data during an experiment

- Using an adventure game, where clues are collected and puzzles solved

- Designing a computer model of a situation or process

- Watching a multimedia CD-ROM presentation

- Creating a computer program using a programming language

- Using software to control the movements of a robot

- Using a decision-making simulation program

- Using Logo to generate and investigate mathematical shapes

- Setting up a database to store and analyse collected information.

Even though IT is now an issue for all teachers, it would be unreasonable to expect familiarity with the whole range of applications. The possibilities may well be daunting to beginning teachers, newly-qualified teachers, or established teachers for whom IT is still a 'grey area'. The advice to such people must be to first become familiar with one or two generic applications, then use these to develop some simple activities for students that can make a clear contribution to learning in the subject area taught. For example, familiarity with a word processor and a graphics program will enable creative activities, such as the production of newspaper articles, letters, poems and reports to which simple illustrations or graphs can be added. Or learning to use a spreadsheet can lead to useful opportunities for data-handling and modelling, such as the entry of survey results for graphing and analysis, or the setting up of a simple financial model for predicting the profits of a company.

There are many sound reasons for starting with generic programs. Virtually every school will have a basic set of generic programs, so investment in training can be built upon and applied in any teaching post. In contrast, each school will have its own peculiar combination of specific programs and valuable time could be wasted learning them. Another reason for concentrating on generic software, is that the IT skills acquired are more transferable and future-proofed. The content-free nature of generic software means it can be applied in a variety of contexts. Also, the nature of generic programs does not change enormously – they just become more sophisticated. Specific programs, on the other hand, tend to have their own idiosyncrasies and the content they carry may well become out-of-date or less appropriate as time goes by. Finally, and most importantly, the use of generic software can make a greater contribution to IT capability. Specific software applications can be added to a teacher's 'repertoire' once general confidence in IT has been established and experience gained in using IT with school students.

Practice in Hampstead School

So, what is happening in IT at Hampstead School? Like most schools following a cross-curricular approach to IT, Hampstead is primarily concerned with developing a range of IT experiences for school students. This is done so that all areas of IT capability can be developed and progress can be made to advanced skills. For example, in English, Year 7 students have produced poems and news-paper articles using a word processor. In one case, a class newspaper was pro-duced by manually cutting and pasting together articles and pictures done by the class. This activity could be developed further by getting students to piece together the various newspaper components on the computer, using a desktop publishing program. Similar activities are done in History, where students reported on an event from the past from a particular viewpoint. Others recently produced news articles reporting on events in Little Rock when schools became desegregated in the 1960s. They also use word processing facilities in French, German and Spanish; for example, they have produced profiles of themselves for imaginary pen-friends. There is scope for the use of the Internet here – some of the older school students have used electronic-mail to communicate with schools in other countries. In French, Year 8 has used a graphics program to create an outline of the human body and then have labelled it in French. Students have opportunities to develop more sophisticated uses of graphics programs in their Design and Technology lessons, where IT is an integral part of all courses.

Data handling is another important element of IT capability that our students are developing, particularly in the use of databases and CD-ROMs to do research for their various projects. In History and Geography, students of all ages are encouraged to use these tools in addition to paper-based research materials, both in and out of lessons. A range of reference tools is available for them to access information on just about any subject. Simple text and picture-based CD-ROMs are easy for us to network and make available to whole classes. The Internet has also proved useful for this – some students have been able to use the World Wide Web to search for up-to-the-minute information and news on various subjects and in different languages. We also have careers databases that students can either browse in a general way, or use to perform searches based on information about their own interests entered via a questionnaire. In addition to the use of existing databases, they are given opportunities to create their own databases using information they have collected themselves. One example is in Geography, where they collect data in a traffic survey and then analyse their results, producing bar charts, pie charts and histograms.

One area of IT that has been difficult for schools to implement is modelling. Much of the work that has been done has focused on the use of spreadsheets as modelling tools. At Hampstead School, students use spreadsheets in their Maths lessons to generate sequences and series, and also to explore formulas. The programming language Logo also provides an excellent modelling environment, particularly for geometry, where students can explore the mathematical rules underlying shapes.

Simulations are also important as pre-modelling activities. School students can use models that have already been created to simulate processes or situations. One good example is a spreadsheet simulation of the water cycle, used in Year 9 Geography classes. Students have control over certain variables that change the effects of a rain storm on a river, such as the type of land, duration and intensity of the storm and so on. After selecting a set of variables they can create a hydrology graph that shows the water level of the river at different times and they can determine whether or not flooding occurs. More complex simulations allow control over the rules of the model, as well as the variables. At the higher levels, they should be able to create their own models for a given situation or process using suitable software. An example from Geography involves drawing possible routes for a new road on a simple map with a grid. The cost of building the road can be estimated by counting the number of squares that the route passes through for different types of land – forest, settlement, marsh and so on. This information is entered on a spreadsheet and formulas entered to calculate the total estimated costs. A simple model is thereby created, which can be used to try out different routes, comparing the costs.

The Design and Technology department at Hampstead involves activities where IT is used to control other simple devices, such as bulbs and motors. In one example, the students make computer controlled traffic lights. The three bulbs (red, amber and green) are controlled from the computer via a special interface box. A flow chart program generates appropriate commands for controlling the lights. In the Science department IT is used to collect data from experiments using sensors. A common experiment involves using temperature sensors, connected to a computer via an interface box, to measure the temperature of hot water at regular intervals as it cools. The software draws a graph of the incoming data, generating a cooling curve. The cooling curves for two different containers, one insulated, can be compared by using two sensors. Portable computers have proved useful when doing this type of experiment – they are easier to set up near the laboratory equipment. Another opportunity for data-logging is offered in PE, where students can monitor their own pulse rates with portable sensors during physical activities. The data is stored within these sensors and can later be transferred to a computer for analysis.

In the examples given above, the intention is for IT to be used to enhance learning within the particular subject as well as for IT capability to be developed. Whether or not this dual aim is achieved can only be judged by observing school students during the activities and from the perceived outcomes of the activities. Different levels of enhancement can be identified when evaluating these activities. In most cases, at the very least, increased student motivation is observed when IT is being used. Frequently, it is clear that the use of IT has enabled students to improve the quality of their presentations. Often, IT can free students from otherwise very laborious tasks and allow them to concentrate on the concepts and skills underlying the particular area of study. Sometimes, the use of IT can lead to a greater understanding or grasp of a particular topic, concept or skill, because of the way in which it has been presented and developed. Occasionally, the use of IT enables learners to see something in a way that they have not experienced before and perhaps would not have experienced at all without the influence of IT. This last type of enhancement is almost magical, and is a very personal experience in the sense that others could find similar 'inspiration' in different circumstances or with different resources. In all of these levels of enhancement, the quality of learning may not be attributable to the use of IT alone. It will be determined by the particular set of factors that make up the teaching-learning situation, of which IT is just one.

The IT department at Hampstead School provides INSET for all staff, at three different levels: general, workshop and departmental. Recent general sessions have included IT for beginners, introductions to word processing and graphics, using a spreadsheet for simple modelling, using data handling programs and a look at how we can use the Internet. In addition to these, workshop sessions are provided, for staff to come along and practise their IT skills with help at hand. Departmental INSET is also offered, so that whole departments can explore uses of IT relating specifically to their curriculum area. Although much high quality INSET is available form LEAs, HEIs and other consultancies, on-site IT training is often more fruitful, as staff can develop skills using the available equipment and immediately share ideas with colleagues. An introductory session is held each year to help beginning teachers to use IT at Hampstead School during their teaching practices. An outline of the facilities available is given and beginning teachers are registered on the school's network, so that they can begin to use and evaluate the resources. They are encouraged to use the facilities to help produce their own classroom materials, as well as to try out IT activities in their lessons. In the past, beginning teachers have also been helped with their university work, using the IT resources to produce essays and present research findings in the form of graphs.

Looking to the future, at Hampstead School we are always looking for new contexts for the learning and application of IT skills, and for new technologies to extend IT capability and enhance subject teaching. We are striving to make these opportunities available to all students as an entitlement. We are also very keen to use IT to promote independent learning – enabling students to take more control of their own learning by giving them access to high-quality materials and tools. The assessment issue is also high on the agenda – we need to devise a cross-curricular system for recording and monitoring of IT skills, so that each student's IT capability can be assessed and rewarded.

Hampstead School is fortunate to be well-equipped, thanks mainly to a successful bid for TSI (Technology Schools Initiative) funding in 1992, but is it ever possible to have enough? There are several major projects planned for the future, that will demand further investment in IT resources. The most ambitious is the expansion of the school library as an independent learning resource centre, possibly for local community access, building on traditional resources with audio-visual materials, IT tools, Internet access, video conferencing facilities and a reprographics centre. The school's existing Internet connections are via stand-alone computers, so access is limited. The need to provide network Internet access is increasingly apparent as more staff and students identify uses for its facilities. Another area of great interest to the school is the use of portable computers, particularly palmtops. The prices of these machines are coming down while their capabilities are increasing, and it is not difficult to envisage a time when all students will be able to own one. We need to evaluate the potential of palmtops as a support to learning. One of the most frightening (but also exciting) aspects of IT is the speed with which it moves on. Schools are no different from business and industry in their desire to make the latest technologies available. However, we have to learn to use the resources we already have properly, building upon them when the time is right.

Finally, beginning teachers at Hampstead School have been able to learn about the use of IT in the context described above and to use our resources in their own school-based research. One beginning teacher learnt to use a data base so that she could process a survey on the languages spoken at Hampstead School, as part of her research for a final course assignment. She then learnt a graphics programme, so that she could prepare for a seminar presentation of her findings. Her resulting display has now been in use for two years in the school. The school tries to encourage beginning teachers to research into areas in which we have expertise, and also in which we would like to see development. An example would be a recent piece of research by a beginning teacher as part of a school-based project, in which he devised a questionnaire to see whether Hampstead students felt that the national curriculum for IT was being successfully delivered and where improvements needed to be made. The results were useful to us and have suggested a further area of research, after we have initiated developments.

Conclusion

The key issues surrounding IT in schools can be summarised with four words: entitlement, enhancement, access and support. In order for students to acquire IT capability, schools have to establish an IT entitlement for all. IT skills need to be learned and applied in a range of curriculum contexts, as an enhancement to learning. Staff and students need easy access to IT facilities, and also support and encouragement from the IT co-ordinator. To make this work IT needs to be every teacher's second subject and a key element in ITET.

CHAPTER 6

SUPPORTING BILINGUAL LEARNERS
Marc Thompson

At Hampstead School there are currently six hundred and four students receiving bilingual support. This is more than half the school population. Some are refugee and asylum seekers and some are more permanently settled. What characterises them for our department is their bilingual needs which we assess when they arrive in school. The Bilingual Support Department's aim is to provide students whose first language is not English with appropriate English language support so that they can have full access to the school curriculum and are able to achieve to the best of their ability. The department, consisting of four full-time teachers, offers in-class support, intensive language development classes and language workshops. A refugee co-ordinator also shares many aspects of the department's work, supporting refugee students, many of whom have their language acquisition hampered by previous traumatic experiences. (For more details of this, c.f. Chapter 7.)

We first meet BTs during their induction period in September, when they shadow a student who has bilingual support for a day. In this way, BTs see in-class support as well as withdrawal groups and observe students within their tutor group. The students who are shadowed are chosen in consultation with the school-based tutor, who organises a follow-up seminar to discuss their observations. The beginning teachers' initial reactions are often characterised by surprise, as the following report demonstrates. This report also gives the flavour of the task and shows how BTs discover some of the issues raised in this chapter. The student shadowed was assessed by us as a Stage 1 learner i.e. 'new' to English: the stages are explained later in the chapter.

Shadowing a Year 7 school student with ESL needs

The day began with a Science lesson. S. was sitting next to her friend, another school student who needs special help due to her English language needs. In the early stages of the lesson, students were engaged with form-filling as part of self-assessment. S. looked as if she was concentrating very hard, with an intense expression, clearly trying to make sense of the task she had been set. Her confused gestures demonstrated to me just how difficult things must be for her, having to grapple with a complex new language, whilst also dealing with the difficulties presented by new processes. Right from the start, S. and her friend were behind the pace of the mainstream class. This meant that they had not completed a task at the close of the session which the majority of the class had left behind at the half- way point. She tried for over half an hour to understand difficult scientific terminology and syntax. Complex words such as 'interpret' meant little to her. Under-developed reading skills create pitfalls and a simple error can render an apparently clear question completely unintelligible. An example of this was when S read 'there' as 'three'. At such an early stage, the concepts of logical analytical thought are difficult to grasp, but along a whole range of formal, specialised language, S has to face a set of problems, which I am sure I would find daunting if I were in her position. I sensed a fierce intelligence trying to assert itself, despite having to operate in a language which is unfamiliar. S's oral expression appears to be well in advance of her written and comprehension skills. Print and the act of writing obviously demand much more than engaging in a conversation.

During the period set aside for English, S and four others attended a special class, aimed at helping those with particular language difficulties. This session was conducted in a very relaxed and informal atmosphere. It was easy to see that such an environment is a god-send for students who have to struggle though most of the day in a formal classroom context. The basis of this class is also social interaction between the students and the teacher. Time was spent on discussion, getting them to share ideas and stories. Once the pressure was lifted, learning became an effortless experience, with skills being acquired without any formal procedures. Such a collaborative and leisurely approach encourages students to engage in using language without the anxiety which is generated by failing to complete a rigid task within a limited time. S. was one of the more reticent students in this session but I sensed that she was using this time to unwind, after the efforts she had made in the earlier lessons.

The experience of shadowing a school student with a limited grasp of the English language has demonstrated to me what a tremendous amount of commitment such students invest. At this moment, when I am acquiring new skills, I can appreciate just how much effort such students make.

Bilingual students – assessment and testing

Primary school children come into Year 7 at Hampstead School with their bilingual background noted on their transfer forms. We consider any child born outside the UK whose first language is not English, or whose parents were born outside the UK. and whose language is not English, as a potential client of the Bilingual Support department.

In September all students from year 7 who are bilingual students and all students in the school on the bilingual register are given a simple language test. Test scores are recorded and, together with teacher's observations, stage scores are given and recorded on the school's database. One of our functions is to provide information on the ESL stages of our students to all teachers in the school. They are required to keep a note of these stages, to ensure that they keep bilingual students' ESL needs in mind when planning differentiation. We provide an information session for beginning teachers on this and on the further services which we offer the school to support students' learning. This information is distributed to all staff by the end of the fourth week of the Autumn Term, in the form of a booklet which lists the students' stages of English, their country of origin and home language. The department follows Hilary Hester's stage guidelines set out in Fig. 6.1, although we further subdivide each stage into a, b, or c to aid us in assessing and monitoring progress in more detail (Hester, 1988).

During the academic year 1995-96, for example, we had a total of 1, 238 students in the school. The figures on bilingual support we sent to the Home Office relating to our funding were:

TOTAL STUDENTS	1238
TOTAL AT STAGE 1	21
TOTAL AT STAGE 2	72
TOTAL AT STAGE 3	147
TOTAL AT STAGE 4	364
TOTAL BILINGUAL STUDENTS	604

The importance of record-keeping

Such figures underline the importance of record-keeping, which we stress to our beginning teachers in their induction period when we show them the value of a systematic and manageable system. In our case, bilingual support teachers record the work they do and make observations about students on 'withdrawal' and 'in-class support' record sheets. Each student's progress is summarised and recorded termly. We make use of a form to help our students in self-assessment for this task. Annual reports are then based on the information contained in the termly reviews and, in the case of those in withdrawal classes, on other monitoring forms, i.e. language acquisition progress forms and ESL curriculum progress forms.

These records are kept in separate files for each bilingual school student and can be consulted by all staff. Ideally these files contain a copy of the Year 7 initial interview form, the induction test, any subsequent tests, termly review forms, a copy of their syllabus progress form (updated termly), the teacher's language progress forms (updated termly), copies of all annual reports, parental contact slips, action request slips from staff, any individual plans supplied by the curriculum support department and samples of work (updated annually). They exclude any confidential information, which remains with the head of year or the refugee co-ordinator. (The issue of confidentiality and how we deal with sensitive issues when briefing beginning teachers is dealt with later in the chapter).

When beginning teachers have been introduced to a bilingual learner in the school and have begun to develop an idea of the range of other educational needs in the school, they are able to approach our department for support and advice. It might then be useful to outline how the department functions, as this is the base from which we are able to support beginning teachers in their immediate work in school and in their further development, through their profiling and research tasks. This academic year, for example, the department offered the following in-class support for Stage 1 and 2 learners, from Year 7 to Year 11. We gave ten periods of support in Maths, ten to Science, seven to English, five to History and five to Geography. Teachers of subjects which do not get support tell us they would like more. However, we have limited resources and have chosen to focus on new arrivals and students at Key Stage 4 .

In addition to in-class support, we have run nine language-development workshops (three in Year 7, two for Years 8 and 9 and two each in Years 10 and 11). We also operate an open door policy for bilingual students at Stage 3 seeking help with any aspect of their school life. Some of the beginning teachers also seek advice on their work and their research tasks and we sometimes find the number of adults in the room outweighs the number of students! However, the beginning teachers can also be roped in to give useful, extra support when required. We encourage beginning teachers to become involved with the work of the department and many come to these workshops.

The BTs we have worked with so far have come from curriculum subject areas. We have not yet trained bilingual support specialists, but we are considering this development, since we could provide good specialist bilingual support training. For example, we offer the Cambridge First Certificate and this year we have twenty students planning to take the examination in the summer. (Over the past three years there has been a 100% success rate at these examinations). Both courses are internationally recognised and are particularly useful for students planning to return to their country of origin in the near future.

Bilingual Support and Special Needs

'Bilingual students are not special needs students!' This was once the clarion call of teachers working in bilingual support and with good reason. Thankfully, bilingual students are no longer considered to have learning difficulties in the remedial sense. However, they do have needs and some may have learning difficulties. The ethos of Hampstead School recognises that the needs of all its students are special to each individual, no matter what their ability or background. National statistics suggest that between 15 and 20 percent of all students have some form of learning difficulty. It might therefore be reasonable to assume the same to be true for bilingual students in addition to their bilingual needs. In fact, at Hampstead School 16.7% of all students have some form of learning difficulty, whilst only 12.3% of bilingual students on ESL stages 1 to 4 have some form of learning difficulty in addition to their bilingual needs (figures for May 1996).The significance of these figures is open to debate. However, it is clear that students' needs cannot easily be pigeon-holed and that effective support involves the Bilingual Support department and Curriculum Support department collaborating closely with other departments, and above all with each other, to assess and meet the needs of the students. Nationally, bilingual learners with special needs have been targeted recently, as a group which the system has failed in the past, and appropriate training is now being offered for both qualified and newly qualified staff (Hall, 1995). One of our recently qualified staff has, in fact, undertaken this training. The school has also targeted a small group of students in Year 7 to support them with both ESL and with their own more general needs for support in accessing the curriculum.

As a school then, we can only provide optimum support across the curriculum by linking and co-ordinating the work of the Bilingual Support and Curriculum Support Departments. Attitudes and opinions vary but I believe that there are far more similarities than differences in the day-to-day mechanics of our work. In developing close links with the Curriculum Support department we have found that we have gained a more even spread of in-class support throughout the school. This has proved particularly successful with those bilingual students who do also have also have other special educational needs. It should also help to streamline the statementing process for any bilingual students who may need to be involved.

Funding and organisation of support

Our work is supported by our LEA and draws upon the expertise and support of the Camden Language and Support Service (CLASS). The department is funded by Camden LEA, who in turn receive their funding from the Home Office Section 11 budget. This form of funding is now ending as Camden, like many other LEA's, is moving over to the Single Regeneration Budget (SRB). Under this funding scheme, bilingual support provision is in direct competition with other Borough services and priorities. Bilingual Support administrators, working with funding allocated from the SRB, have found to their cost that the old Section 11 funding was both greater and more reliable. Our funding is generated from the data on the stages of bilingual students, which we gain through our testing procedures. This is sent to Camden LEA in November and used for funding allocation under Section 11. Based on the resulting budget we could allocate support and establish withdrawal classes. However, the changes in forms of support have yet to be worked through and the future still looked uncertain at the time this chapter was written.

Just as funding arrangements are changing, so there has been an on-going debate over the past few years over the withdrawal of bilingual students from lessons, particularly to language centres. Withdrawal off-site has often been a cheaper, and in some ways, a convenient way of giving support for the development of English language, but it has been shown that students learn English more effectively by working among English-speaking students and by actively engaging in mainstream activities. We believe at Hampstead School that the language of the normal mainstream classroom does offer the best context for learning language, because the bilingual students are learning English for the purpose of learning the subject being taught, and not in the abstract. Because group activities involve discussion, students can learn by listening to other students and by relating the discussion to what they see happening. They learn language in context, which is how language is most effectively learnt. They are offered a motivating experience to learn English in wanting to join in the activities of their peers, both inside and outside lessons. As Jill Rutter puts it:

> If bilingual students are withdrawn from the mainstream, whether into language centres or withdrawal groups, all these incentives to learn English are removed. Additionally, the only model of correct English the bilingual school student will hear will be the teacher's, because all the other students will have limited English. Most importantly, bilingual students will not have the same full access to the curriculum as other students (Rutter, 1994, p. 71).

A further reason for keeping withdrawal to the minimum, is that developing the English of bilingual students should be seen as the responsibility of all teachers. This is the position we also adopt on the development of IT skills and on the education of students with special educational needs. (c.f. Chapters 4 and 5). If students are withdrawn for too many of their lessons, this language development may then be seen to be solely the responsibility of the support teacher. We welcome the advantages of working in collaboration with classroom teachers in the mainstream and feel that we are able to encourage classroom teachers to develop skills in English language support.

However, we do withdraw students at Stage 1, to provide them with basic skills, working to a planned syllabus. These withdrawal lessons take place three times a week and we re-integrate students when the bilingual support teacher and the subject teacher feel it is appropriate. I would like to say that most students return to mainstream classes after one academic year. However, this is not always the case and some students need continued withdrawal and it was encouraging that the department was able to stop its Year 8 Stage 2 withdrawal class after only one term this year.

In establishing any withdrawal class, whether long or short term, the department only responds to generally agreed need on the part of the students.

The withdrawal is always minimal 3 lessons in a 20 lesson week is the maximum and if there is any doubt whether withdrawal lessons are needed, they are not offered. All students are also welcome at our homework clubs, where further support is given after school.

Withdrawal is part of an ongoing debate in bilingual support teaching, which we try to reveal to our beginning teachers. We expect them to see the full extent of our work with students and to understand how our work relates to the rest of the curriculum. For example, developing IT skills has become an integral part of all withdrawal classes. Chapter 5 has described the school's philosophy that every teacher needs to teach IT skills and that all students have a right to certain entitlement activities. To help in this, the Bilingual Support department's net-worked base room has four PCs which were networked in September 1996, two of which have multimedia capabilities. In addition to word processing, the department integrates a variety of software to develop basic skills into its with-drawal classes, as well as offering computer access to all bilingual students at lunch time, after school and during homework clubs. The general knowledge CD ROMs such as *Encarta* and the Kingfisher *Micropeadia* have proved valuable to our students researching homework topics and projects.

We believe withdrawal classes to be a very valuable experience for some students. This is endorsed by the following, taken from another beginning teacher's report of shadowing a bilingual school student for a day. Two lessons only are reported here, with the beginning teacher's comments. The bilingual school student is represented as A:

> I cannot possibly begin to comprehend the feeling of complete isolation that must be present when you are put into a classroom full of students and they're all talking at you and you cannot understand a single word they are saying. Registration was the normal whirl of events It happened so fast that I nearly missed it. A seemed to be part of a group. Period 1 was Science and the topic was adaptations. A was sitting alone and was very quiet. Does he have no friends or were they in a different lesson?. He was shy and reserved. The only school student-school student interaction I observed was hostile, caused by the prospect of sharing a book with a girl. Even during a class discussion, A remained quiet and dreamy. The only time he did what he was told, was to copy the others. Was this because he was not listening, or was it because he did not understand? During the course of the morning I dis-covered it was a mixture of both....
>
> Period 2 was English. A went to a withdrawal lesson, along with five other students from his year. The difference in A was unimaginable. He was a part of the class. He was making helpful comments and suggestions and obviously really enjoying the lesson. He had not done his homework because, so he claimed, he had not understood it. The teacher gave a brief explanation and he was then able to do it in five minutes. The students were

far more relaxed, due to the teacher's informal approach. This was possible as there were only 7 in the class. Perhaps A's change in behaviour was a direct result of the small class size, given in a friendly and less intimidating environment, especially as all the students were bilingual learners.

Overall A is a very intelligent child, who is just getting to grips with the English language. I think that he is being taught in the best way possible. He would miss out on too much if he were to be withdrawn from all lessons, even though he has language difficulties. Perhaps more support in the form of a language assistant could be given, but the funding to provide this, for even the most needy of cases, would be immense.

This student is clearly thinking carefully about the advantages and disadvantages of withdrawal over in-class support.

A further way in which beginning teachers can learn about withdrawal classes is by looking through the records which teachers of withdrawal groups keep. At the end of each term, teachers summarise what they have done in withdrawal classes, noting what worked well and the resources used and beginning teachers have found such information useful and informative.

Advice and support

Every fourth week, all members of the department meet with the refugee co-ordinator and a specialist from the Tavistock Clinic (child psychology unit) to discuss individual refugee students, their problems and progress. These sessions were instigated by the school to provide ongoing appropriate training for the department's members. Due to the sensitive nature of the issues discussed and the need for confidentiality, beginning teachers and NQTs wishing to sit in or to contribute do need to approach the refugee co-ordinator for a special invitation.

As one beginning teacher wrote in one of her assignments:

> ...emotional support is of a very personal nature and is only available when there is trust between two people. This development of trust is a key issue when the emotional needs of a child are to be assessed. It takes a great deal of time for a traumatised child to develop a trusting relationship with any-one. It appears as though there is very little emotional support outside school.

While we can give beginning teachers a taste of the issues involved, we cannot share with them particular information about students. In this sense they have a very intimate view of the school but cannot share fully all the information which may be accessed by members of staff.

Beginning teachers in their classrooms

Beginning teachers face their first tests of planning and curriculum delivery when they need to produce lesson plans for whole lessons. This occurs around the third week of their first teaching practice, since they will have been gently eased into the task by first observing whole lessons, then working on team-taught elements of a lesson. Advice on work to support bilingual learners can also be gained within their curriculum departments from experienced teachers, particularly from 'link teachers' who are specified teachers in each department with responsibility for liaison with our department. We also have specified links ourselves with Maths, Science, English, Geography and History and suitably differentiated materials are being produced on a regular basis, in collaboration with each department. To further this collaboration, all teachers in the Bilingual Support department are attached to year teams, providing a vital link with the pastoral programme and year team system. In this connection, we have, for example, produced a list of students able and willing to translate for parents and new students and we organise translators for parents' evenings when required.

Conclusion

During the first few weeks of their time in school beginning teachers will have been introduced to the needs of bilingual students, through the shadowing exercise and to issues raised by these needs, such as planning for differentiation. They will have reflected on this shadowing exercise, learnt the rationale for recording the bilingual students' ESL stages on their school mark sheet, learnt where to find the information to be recorded and who to consult when planning

---

Figure 6. 1

TIPS AND BITS WORTH REMEMBERING

WITHDRAWAL LESSONS

- Provide a whole class introduction.
- Include an interactive/group work aspect.
- Focus on a language point.
- Give individual attention where possible.
- Have individual work/syllabi where necessary.
- Try to personalise e.g. culturally, some aspect of the work for each student.
- Check on cross-curricular progress

lessons. In addition they have been instructed to keep their information up to date, as must all teaching staff in the school, by regularly consulting the staff notice board on which we display the latest information on our work. In fact, the good practice which we try to encourage in the beginning teachers at this school is no different from the procedures we demand of all teachers in this area. New and old teachers alike, for example are encouraged to think particularly of their bilingual students and to keep a hint list (c.f. Fig 6.2) in their folder for planning withdrawal lessons.

We already have an ever-increasing differentiated resource bank for subject areas, which has been developed with the Curriculum Support department and teachers from the subject areas concerned. We have also organised a programme of three INSET days per year, per key subject area, for developing differentiated schemes of work. It can been seen then, that a great deal of the Bilingual Support department's work is as a resource centre for all teachers, as well as teaching bilingual students directly. We believe that all teachers in the school support bilingual learners and that good quality training and inset should be available to all.

CHAPTER 7

REFUGEE EDUCATION: ONE IN EVERY CLASS

Ruth Heilbronn

He came from Somalia. He had seen his father shot and his mother and sister killed by a grenade. He fled his country, his home, for fear of being killed himself. He is now here in London, seeking asylum. The saddest part of his story is that he is not alone. This is all too familiar amongst the refugee students at Hampstead School.

The term refugee, as defined by the 1955 UN Convention, is someone who has fled from his or her home country, or is unable to return to it 'owing to a well-founded fear of being persecuted for reasons of race, religion, nationality, membership of a particular social group or political opinion.'

There are over 150 refugee students at Hampstead School and nearly a third of these are unaccompanied. This means that they have no family with them. A young boy of 13 fled from his country with a 'family friend' i.e. someone whom the family paid to take the child to a safe place. He was dumped in the middle of the night at Islington underground station. He was alone in a country miles from his own land, having witnessed the most horrendous events, and the government told him he must go to school and study the national curriculum just like every other child. But he is not like every other child. How can education be important to refugee students when they have barely escaped with their lives? How can we as teachers educate them, make them feel welcome, try to help them through their trauma? The simple answer is that we cannot easily do so.

These comments come from the introduction to a research project undertaken by a beginning teacher at the school and indicate her difficulty in coming to terms with the problems she felt as a mainstream teacher of groups which included refugees.

The one hundred and fifty refugee or asylum-seeking students the beginning teacher mentions, represent about ten percent of our school population. Many are from Eritrea and Somalia and from ex-Yugoslavia, among them a number of unaccompanied refugee children. This is not untypical of some London schools, as by far the majority of refugees and asylum seekers in Britain are in London (some 90% of those resident in Great Britain today, although accurate data is difficult to come by). In March 1994 it was estimated by the Refugee Council that there were approximately 22,000 refugee students in London. Nearly every school in inner London has refugee students and some schools have numbers similar to ours. Nor is it a recent phenomenon. It is sometimes difficult for beginning teachers to grasp the implications of all this. We then try to educate our beginning teachers by first sketching out the traditional response of London schools to the cultural pluralism of their populations over the past few years and by pointing to some of the initiatives, particularly by the former Inner London Education Authority in this field, where some excellent work in multi-cultural education was done. However, as this chapter will show, we also begin the process which continues in their teaching practice, of showing our beginning teachers how the needs of the refugee students differ from those of previous immigrant arrivals, with extra dimensions which need to be addressed before we can meet their educational needs. These issues are the focus of this chapter and a useful starting point is the context within which the school works.

Local authorities in London have to deal with an increasing range of refugee needs within a shrinking resource base. Despite this dwindling resource base, many local authorities in greater London are concerned about the level of service that they provide to refugees and asylum seekers, especially those of school age. Evidently, what is needed for such students and their families is a multi-agency, integrated approach to refugee issues, with co-ordination in the welfare system between the agencies concerned with the individual refugee and also co-ordination between these welfare agencies and school and refugee community groups. The London Borough of Camden, our LEA, has dealt with this need in several ways. It has:

- held a conference which aimed to develop an understanding of refugee students' educational needs; to provide information about refugee students' backgrounds and to provide a framework for those who have management responsibility for meeting the educational needs of refugee students

- produced a Refugee Education Policy to meet the educational needs of refugee students

- begun to bring its various agencies and departments together through the creation of a Refugee Education Project Co-ordinator, whose vital role is one of liaison, education, support and development to schools in the area.

The Camden Language and Support Service, under whose umbrella the Refugee Co-ordinator works, has also issued important advice on welfare and legislation issues, as for example during the academic year 1995/96 when the Asylum and

Immigration Act was going through Parliament. This legislation had a major impact on our refugee students and the information circulated was necessary to inform teachers, so that they could effectively support students. So, for example, we were alerted to look out for changes in our refugee students, among which might be attendance patterns, such as students unexpectedly disappearing from school registers, change in health due to poor diet, lack of food, poor housing conditions and homelessness resulting in malnutrition and susceptibility to diseases associated with poverty. We were made aware of the need to set up a hardship fund, to compensate for students unable to claim free school meals.

Throughout the various initiatives that our school has undertaken, advice and support has been co-ordinated by the Camden Refugee Education Project Co-ordinator. She also supports and monitors our own co-ordinator, since the LEA has also created a new post for a school-based refugee co-ordinator. This has been filled by a teacher at our school, currently a year Head. Among other initiatives, the school's refugee co-ordinator has brought together a group of teachers and volunteers from the sixth form of the school, who run an after-school club to support refugee and asylum seekers with school work. This has turned out to be a place where learning goes on in unexpected ways, with the helpers often gaining as much or more than those they are supporting. Students doing A level French for example, have produced successful coursework assign-ments comparing and contrasting the situation for asylum-seekers in France and Britain. Beginning teachers have also chosen to do research-based coursework in this area, as a direct result of helping out at the after-school club. (An offshoot of the after-school club has been the establishment of a charity 'Children of the Storm', run by volunteer helpers, to raise funds and administer grants for basic necessities for these students and their families. This work will be discussed in more detail later in the chapter).

Supporting beyond the curriculum

Students and beginning teachers helping at the club come to understand that many of the school's refugee students have had traumatic experiences. In addition, many have difficulties in daily survival, particularly those unaccom-panied refugee young people who have arrived in this country without parents or guardians. Some have been sent out of a war-zone with a grandparent or an elderly relation, who may need as much support to cope with their new life as the young refugee. The young person may have to become the principle organiser of social and welfare matters. Such young people require a great deal of support in relation to housing, health and a wide range of legal issues relating to their status and they need a great deal of tutor time to help them relate to the various agencies. We have found that our school and others in London, are doing far more than just educating these young people. We frequently find ourselves trying to fill up gaps in the welfare net: for example, staff rally round to find the basics of home sustenance. They organise furniture removal, paying the costs themselves, to have items such as mattresses and bedding, kitchen tables and chairs, cookers and fridges put in their refugee and asylum-seeking students' accommodation. They undertake home visits and sometimes even provide basic foodstuffs. Often staff of the school may be the child's only negotiator and mediator with British bureaucracy.

With the presence of a refugee education co-ordinator in the school, an initiative has been to set up a tutor group intended for those refugee students who are in Year 10 and above, but who are not yet able to participate in the full school curriculum. Launched in 1995, it has eight students at present. The purpose of the initiative, is to provide these students with the language and learning skills they need to benefit from the education system in this country. In addition to language difficulties, most have experienced interruptions to their previous education in their home countries and have often faced severe disturbances and distress due to war or persecution. One of their basic needs must be to have the barriers which block their effective entry to the school curriculum broken down (Jones, 1993, Rutter, 1994).

The work of the refugee co-ordinator has been key in this area. She has been able to liaise between departments and to put together an educational package of courses for her tutor group, which will facilitate their integration later into the school system and make pathways for progression into higher education. As part of this programme, the group is integrated into years 11 and 12 for Maths, all do Science with Year 11, follow the Youth Award Scheme in line with years 10 and 12, do Basketball and PE with Year 12 students, and work as a group together in English, Information Technology, European History and Art. In addition, two students from former Yugoslavia, who lived in France before coming to Britain, are following the A-level French course and two others are following the A-Level Maths course.

There is then much of interest and importance for beginning teachers to experience in this area. Refugee students living in London have particular educational needs, which teachers must address in their planning for differentiated work. It will now be evident why we insist on early induction in this area for beginning teachers. Having understood the general context and then the school context, they are in a position to learn about the specific, identified educational needs for these students In this learning process they are like any teacher new to our school, no matter how long s/he has been teaching, in their need for general induction. We can, for instance, give them specific information to guide them, such as the following, taken from interviews with Eritrean refugee students in Sweden, who were asked specifically what they liked about their school. They said that they liked teachers who made some adjustment to their teaching methods, recognising that their past experiences were of a more formal education system. They also liked teachers with clear and high expecta-tions; teachers who asked them about themselves, who took racism seriously and who made an effort to include their experiences in the curriculum. (There is some useful information for teachers on this area in Rutter (1994), and in Melzak and Warner (1992) which we advise all our beginning teachers to read.

Of course, critical to the learning of most refugee students is the process of English as a Second Language (ESL). Since the 1980s, we have experienced an increasing political dimension to the funding of this provision. In addition, a survey carried out by the Refugee Council in 1991 showed that expenditure on ESL provision in London schools had not increased in that financial year in proportion to the increased number of refugee children arriving in London LEAs. Indeed, in some London LEAs, funding for ESL has actually decreased in real terms, an issue discussed earlier in Chapter 6.

In that chapter we showed that we introduced beginning teachers to the needs of our bilingual refugee learners by a shadowing exercise. During this exercise we try to give them one refugee student to follow through the day. The beginning teachers are usually shocked by the hurdles which have to be negotiated in school, even in a school which has good policies and practices in place. They recognise the resourcing issue from the outset and their written reports on the exercise often state this in no uncertain terms. Even at this early stage in their teaching life, they manage to see how much work has to be done with little resources and they feel how much more could and should be achieved. One beginning teacher observed in a piece of written feedback: 'We can only do so much to help the refugee children to feel secure...in many schools this is not economically viable and fund-raising events are needed to find the money to support students'.

The language issue is not just an ESL issue (Levine, 1981; Baker, 1988). Students also need opportunities to maintain their mother tongue and links with their home community, both for their emotional support and for cognitive growth (Baside, 1965). The concept-formation and cognitive learning which they will be achieving in school, through English language, will be less developed in many subjects, particularly humanities, than the level they have reached in their own language. Therefore, they need opportunities to continue to develop, with adults as well as their peers, in their own home language. As an example, Somali students have benefited from language support offered through local Somali community organisations and developing links between schools and the community organisations which support students in this respect is a vital area of work. We have drawn on some very useful work on mother-tongue maintenance by the Minority Rights Group's *Voices* Project which has among its other pioneering work over several years, collected and published a series of dual language testimonies written by refugee children in London schools (Warner, 1991a, 1991b). We have subsequently made similar collections in school and held readings by the school student authors of their work. (For a detailed discussion of the issue see Finlay and Reynolds, 1987). Community organisations are vital then, not merely for the emotional and practical support they can give but also educationally, for the links they allow the students to maintain with their home culture and language. However, while schools understand the necessity for creating and maintaining links between them and the various community organisations which support their students, they rarely have the resources to do this effectively.

During their induction period, discussed in Chapter 2, beginning teachers from the Institute of Education often consult with those community organisations in Camden which are relevant to the study they are undertaking. In some ways this gives them a wider conception of the school than some qualified teachers from other areas, who on appointment come straight into their work with students, without this kind of induction period.

More immediately apparent to our beginning teachers is the awareness that refugee students may have undergone deeply scarring personal experiences, as the account at the beginning of this chapter illustrates. In fact, although many London teachers have experience in dealing with a wide range of pastoral issues, the experiences of some of the refugee students are most likely to be outside the daily knowledge of most teachers. Trauma can often manifest itself long after the refugee student has apparently settled into her or his new life. It can cause a variety of behavioural and emotional difficulties and we therefore make sure that our beginning teachers are informed early on, through a formal meeting with the Refugee Co-ordinator, reinforced by the school tutor, of the need to approach students with discretion and understanding.

During the initial induction period beginning teachers will have met with a senior teacher in charge of pastoral work. An initial series of pointers relating to students' behaviour will have been given and the importance of confidentiality in dealing with sensitive information will have been stressed. This alerts them to such issues and gives the legal framework for their obligations as teachers. To help with this we give them a session on the Children Act. Beginning teachers, like newly qualified teachers, do need to be reminded that they will meet many problems among their students which they cannot solve and that, as teachers, they will need to keep clear in their minds their own boundaries as professionals. We have to remind them throughout the course that a teacher's job is primarily to educate students and that we cannot take on the responsibilities more appropriate to the role of a social worker or other professional counsellor. Understanding the need to refer students promptly in certain cases is vital here, i.e. beginning teachers when they first come to their teaching role need to be told clearly and in a formal situation about professional teaching relationships and the need to refer a student through the school's referral systems and procedures, if sensitive and personal information has been disclosed.

In addition to the issue of trauma, beginning teachers, like all other teachers in the school, need to know that there are significant numbers of unaccompanied refugee children who frequently require support to help them cope. Luckily the school has the services of trained child psychotherapists from the Tavistock Clinic, which is near to the school. Several members of staff have done counselling courses with the Tavistock and a child psychotherapist meets regularly with staff who have individual concerns about students. The Tavistock Clinic also facilitates group counselling sessions, which run in the school. If a refugee student cannot cope with group counselling and requires it, s/he is offered individual counselling at the Tavistock Clinic.

The beginning teacher's research quoted at the beginning of the chapter focused on the pastoral support offered to refugee students. In the sense that pastoral support was the major focus of this work, the beginning teacher also came to comprehend some of the basic principles of pastoral work. In tutorials with the school professional tutor, the rationale for these procedures and the system for monitoring consistency by the senior executive team is explained.

As a result of these experiences BTs learn about the pastoral system in the school, including the referral procedures and they develop an understanding of their place in the wider school community, including where they must go for help and support for an individual student. By focusing on refugee issues we can then also draw out the common pastoral concerns which enable us to prepare them for the pastoral role they will take on when they become form tutors in their first job. When the probationary year was in force teachers doing probation did not usually become form tutors and therefore had a year to ease themselves into this role. Many NQTs do now become form tutors in their first year and preparing them for this role is a responsibility for all involved in ITET.

Keeping alert to the work to be done

It will be evident from the issues discussed above that one essential is to inform our own staff and to keep the relevant issues to the forefront of our school agenda. The ICIS study (Rutter and Jones, 1997) showed that teachers in school wished for detailed information about the countries from which their refugee students came, for example, details about the history, languages and religious and schooling system in the countries of origin and the reasons that have led people to seek asylum in Britain. As a result of staff demand in this area, our school held an INSET day in September 1992, organised by the school with outside agencies, including the Tavistock Clinic, the Refugee Council and the Camden Language and Support Service. As is usual with such events, our beginning teachers were encouraged to attend and take a full part in the day's discussions. Folders of up-to-date information on the backgrounds of our refugee school students and the areas from which they had come were prepared and given to every department in the school. Discussion centred on topics previously identified by the organisers. These were, the induction of new students, curriculum implications, classroom management issues for differentiated learning, communications with home and within school, and impact on teachers and pastoral care. As a result of information gathered and pooled on that day, several initiatives were set up. An induction programme for refugee students was developed, during which good induction practice was identified and defined as essential for all school students new to the school. Our induction session and initial school documentation form was redesigned for *all* students as it was generally agreed that good practice in this area had to include all newcomers. Focusing on the needs of our refugee students made us improve our practice for all. We welcomed this salutary message that in planning and pastoral care, good practice must be transferable.

In our curriculum discussions, we decided our current practice of presenting positive images of migration and combating any lurking deficit model of education implied by the large number of refugee students in our school. Further, curriculum mapping (i.e. departments were asked to identify where they covered these aspects in their curriculum and this information was centralised in the form of a 'curriculum map') followed this induction day so that we could decide related issues. Through subjects such as history, geography and English all our students are taught about refugees, who they are and why they have come to Britain. In addition, the languages department draws on the diversity of languages in the school and the students' linguistic experience in their language awareness course, using materials developed by London school teachers (Garson, Heilbronn et al, 1989). Our PSHE curriculum also tackles human rights, racism, bullying and bereavement.

We stress to our beginning teachers and staff alike that we welcome the diversity represented by our school population. It has been a tenet of good practice in many schools that refugee students are an enrichment to the community and not a problem. We reject a negative model of bilingual learners which is unfortunately still in force in some areas of the educational establishment.

Conclusion

Regrettably the resources necessary to undertake this work are being stretched, not least because of our new statutory obligations to deliver what some see as a narrowed curriculum. It has been said that:

> ...at the very time that the greatest numbers of refugee school students were being admitted to British schools (1989-92) central government was engaged in making sweeping changes in the education system and challenging many of the progressive education policies introduced in the previous 25 years. The National Curriculum prescribes much of what is taught in school and is arguably more Eurocentric than the previous curricula of many schools. It places greater stress on assimilation and on a single 'British' culture and allows less scope for teaching about the achievements of African and Asian peoples (Rutter, 1994, p.49).

All the issues and initiatives discussed so far have been a fruitful source of study for beginning teachers in their course assignments, some of which require action research. These have required close investigation of practices and of curriculum development and delivery, as well as liaison across the school, with a variety of departments. As such they have helped to consolidate the beginning teachers' general learning about the wider issues in the school.

Finally, it is worth returning to the starting point of this chapter, namely that refugee students are a permanent feature of London's schools. Whether their needs have been adequately met in the past is far from clear. Certainly the training of teachers in the past took little note of them. The partnership system we operate today means that our beginning teachers are made aware of the issues involved and are given insights into what they can do to ensure that such students are given an appropriate education.

SECTION TWO:
INDIVIDUALS LEARNING

CHAPTER 8

BEGINNING TEACHERS AS RESEARCHERS

Crispin Jones

The Area-Based partnership scheme between Camden schools and the Institute of Education (c.f. Chapters 3 and 12) was based on the principle that ITET should have a strong research orientation. Belief in the integral place of research was supported by another principle, that schools like Hampstead are both teaching and researching institutions, like university departments of education. The new form of partnership, it was hoped, would lead to BTs being made aware of their own and the school's existing skills in this area and also help them to develop these skills in a systematic and effective manner. It was also hoped that developing these skills would help to generate and to make more explicit the existing research cultures in the school. This was based on the belief that good educational research often comes from intimate study and reflection on school practice undertaken by a partnership of teachers and their H.E. colleagues, working more formally as researchers.

Several pieces of research were built into the course, first an area-based study followed by a school-based enquiry, a research and development project and a final assignment. As the beginning teachers moved through their course in the school the research element in the work led them to continually question us, the so-called experts, i.e. the teachers from the school and the Institute of Education. It was particularly fascinating and rewarding for all involved to experience the deepening understanding of the processes of schooling gained by the beginning teachers in the course of their year on the PGCE. Through questioning our practices, complex and sophisticated research questions were being investigated by the end of the year by the beginning teachers. Seeing this development convinced us that putting a greater research focus into school- based work had paid off, for the beginning teachers as well as those working with them in the school and the Institute of Education.

This focus was there from the start of the course in relation to what we called the Area Study, when the beginning teachers were asked to research, in small groups, the school's educational and social context. The exercise had two main purposes, to demonstrate the importance to their teaching of knowing such a context and to give them insights into working amid research groups. The BT's may have had little experience of this kind of research, which they would be trying to develop with the students they were teaching.

The exercise had other purposes too. The Institute of Education still recruits relatively few students who have been educated in inner city comprehensive schools, although all staff at the Institute of Education would welcome more of them. This is in itself unremarkable as many such schools send relatively few people on to university. Similarly, the Institute of Education, in the centre of multicultural London, still recruits far fewer potential teachers from ethnic minorities than it would like. Although it is rare for Institute of Education beginning teachers coming from the white British communities to be unaware of issues of racism, prejudice and xenophobia, few have had the experience of dealing with the consequences of these social malaises or of discussing them with fellow beginning teachers from black and other minority communities.

We were lucky in that each year our groups contained beginning teachers who had been through inner city schools and/or were from black and other minority communities. They provided much needed information and, perhaps most importantly, often challenged broad generalisations made by other members of the group. For example, it was all too frequently assumed that such beginning teachers would be politically left-wing, which was by no means invariably the case. Indeed, the complex intermingling of educational issues effected by factors such as class, gender and race proved to be a thread that ran through the year's course, with agreement rarely being achieved. This was both a reflection of the school and also the mix of beginning teachers: it was also a natural way of inspiring research questions and enquiries. 'If you believe that, where is your evidence?' and variations on this question, were an encouraging, albeit challenging theme throughout the year.

Initially, the beginning teachers were sent in small groups of twos and threes on urban trails to the North of the Institute of Education to make them aware of the sudden changes in the urban environment that can occur over very short distances. From the faded splendours of Bloomsbury and the London University precinct to the homelessness, drug-dealing and prostitution in the area around Argyle Square near Kings Cross Station is a only a ten minute walk. The area is full of other contrasts too, such as the new, grandiloquent British Library near run-down housing estates, where racism is a real presence. The beginning teachers found these trails fascinating and talked for hours about what they had seen and what they thought it meant to them and to the task of teaching. They worried about being cultural voyeurs and many admitted that they had never really believed that inner city areas could be as poverty stricken as these appeared to be. More, for the first time for some, they began to have some contexts for some of the school students they might be teaching.

A week or so later, and still at a very early stage in their course, the beginning teachers did another urban trail, this time in relation to the school. Again a route was given them, showing the complex diversities, of people, culture, income, land use and architectural style that surround most inner London secondary schools. They were encouraged to go into the shops to get a feel for the area, buy the local newspapers and read the small ads in the shop windows. After the trail, the groups met in the school, to share their experiences with Institute of Education and school staff. They had learned much, some new to the Institute of Education and school staff. For example, Hampstead, as mentioned in an earlier chapter (Chapter 2), is in the Cricklewood area of London, home to a large community of Irish people. One beginning teacher had bought a range of newspapers that served this and other minority communities in the area. The group were both amazed at the range of community newspapers and also by their own lack of knowledge of many of the major news items covered by the papers. The heterogeneity of the city and its school population became more real. It certainly became more confusing.

Discussions in the school and at the Institute of Education were focused on the importance or otherwise of the urban context of the school students' learning. Most of the beginning teachers wanted to find out more. A range of potential topics was raised, including:

- Demography: who lives here and where they live

- Linguistic issues: who speaks what and where do they speak it

- Economic issues: what work is done in Camden and what work do Camden people do

- Migration and movement patterns: into Britain, into London, across London

- Shops/street markets: corner shops etc

- Religion and faith communities in the area

- Transport issues and their significance for the lives of local young people: bus, tube, train, roads, canal, etc

- Law, order, deviance, crime, all in relation to young people

- Housing: the relationship between local housing patterns and the demographic make up of the school

- The literature of Camden: the 'soft city' of lived experience

- The art of Camden

- Health issues in Camden, particularly in relation to young people, e.g. drugs, HIV/AIDS

- Council functions and local politics in Camden: for example, what does the LEA actually do?

- Adult and children's leisure activities and local play facilities.

We were surprised at the range of topics thrown up by the discussions. It had been agreed that no topic could be investigated by less than three people, to enable coverage in sufficient depth (the time frame was very tight) and to explore the dynamics of group work. It also had the unexpected bonus of throwing beginning teachers together in new combinations, from which strong friendships (and occasionally the reverse) were to flow.

The small groups were set to work. They had to organise their own research, allocate tasks and produce a final report for the rest of the group. In some years, the presentation was followed by a more public display at the Institute of Education of all the groups' work. This was later scaled down, for although very impressive it was felt that the major time involvement involved in presentation for such an important exhibition could be better spent on actual research. It also had the effect of placing extra demands on the Art and Design beginning teachers, who were, in most cases, already expert in presentational skills. Presentations of findings were also made to the beginning teachers' group within each school and these were always fascinating occasions. An example might be helpful to explain this.

In a small classroom at the top of the school, a group of beginning teachers are getting ready to present their research findings to fellow beginning teachers and some teachers whose free period coincides with the presentation. One group has explored the range of religions practised in the area; another, the leisure facilities available to young people in the area; a third has explored the linguistic diversity of the area and compared it with the linguistic diversity found within the school. They have also wrestled with the idea that the area surrounding Hampstead School is not necessarily the same as the area lived in by the school students. In urban schools in London, the idea of a discrete catchment area seldom works. So the question emerges as to what is a comprehensive school,- in what ways is it comprehensive, in what ways is it not?

Such questions remain for discussion on another occasion. For the present, the detail and the insights in the beginning teachers' presentations show that some have invested much time and effort into their enquiry and learned much from it. They have also learned that working in groups, a pedagogic practice that we constantly tell them to foster and encourage in their own teaching, is more difficult than it sounds. One of the group has a part-time job that makes it difficult to meet the other members in non-timetable time; another has child care responsibilities. Careful time planning of these off-course activities has been overturned by the unforeseen time demands of working in such a small research group.

There are other things to be learned. A member of one of the groups sees little value in the exercise and does little for it: the others begin to understand the lack of sanction that they will have as a teacher when faced with similar lack of enthusiasm in the classroom. The discussion of this is surprisingly rewarding. The atmosphere is warm and supportive, so the dissenting beginning teacher is able to expand his views and the other members of his group are able to discuss the issue in a less involved way then they perhaps had done as a group before this session. There is no resolution but there is greater understanding for all of us.

But the positive lessons outnumber the seemingly negative ones. Many have found information which will prove useful the moment that they step into a class in the school. They know more about the backgrounds of the young people that they will be teaching and they certainly know more about the difficulties in initiating and sustaining group work. Those on the other side of the fence, the teachers and Institute of Education tutor, have learned too. We all know more about the area around the school, the backgrounds of some of the students, have been given new insights into the difficulties that we all face when doing group work with those students and have been reminded of our own capacity as teacher researchers. Perhaps it comes as no surprise that we are learning from beginning teachers, for many of them are the products of the learning revolution that has been taking place in our schools over the last thirty or so years, a revolution that has its most recent manifestation in the GCSE.

Although politicians may argue about the raising or declining of standards revealed in GCSE and A Level results, one major, often unacknowledged, beneficial consequence of changes in public examinations over the last few years has been the increased facility with which young people undertake research. New courses which encourage collecting and assessing evidence, in small scale research at school and university, have meant that many young people entering teaching already have a research background. although they may not recognise it as such. Similarly, the new types of teaching that GCSE in particular has encouraged have meant that many teachers in the partnership schools, as in other schools, have had to hone their existing research skills.

The key word here is 'existing'. Teaching has always been, in the hands of its better exponents, a research exercise. Teachers are constantly theorising and testing their theories. A lesson is itself a piece of action research. How and why do my school students learn? Why do they not learn? Why do they misbehave? In many urban schools like Hampstead, these research questions are constantly in most teachers' minds, even if seldom explicit. There are no educational equivalents of a free lunch in such schools. This constant but creative questioning is what helps make the school such an excellent place to train teachers. The beginning teachers from the Institute of Education, who have been trained under the evolving partnership arrangements, have thus been in a research and enquiry culture in both institutions. This has meant that, when working effectively, there has been a breaking down of the research, theory and practice divisions that have often bedevilled initial teacher education and training in previous years.

As the Area Based study had demonstrated, the school context became worthy of study, alongside the beginning teachers' other needs. During the early stages of the course many of their concerns revolved around the perennial issues that beginning teachers face, questions like:

'Can I make my subject meaningful to pupils?'

'Will they listen?'

'What will I do if they don't?'

To ignore such questions is clearly foolish. To be obsessed by them is equally so. Being in school, talking to departmental mentors from an early stage, clearly helped in relation to these issues as did the support and guidance of their Institute of Education tutors. What was new in the partnership was the fact that a designated senior member of school staff, the school-based tutor, and an Institute of Education tutor, both took additional responsibility for the beginning teachers' induction into the classroom. The Area Study had shown them that immediate concerns could be illuminated by a more reflexive attitude, in which research was an active ingredient. To support this there was a weekly meeting of the school's beginning teachers with the school-based tutor, other relevant school staff and the Institute of Education tutor. The agenda was closely tied to the beginning teachers' concerns, mediated by the school's concerns and those of the Institute of Education. Increasingly significantly, it was also concerned with the then new imperatives set by the various demands made on teacher education by a central government anxious to have a clear set of knowledge, understandings and competences for its beginning teachers.

The atmosphere of the seminars was usually relaxed and lively. The weekly meetings had advantages over the more traditional subject groupings of beginning teachers, in Institute curricular groups or school departments. The school was known to all, most knew many of the same pupils and certainly many of the same teachers. They had gradually become familiar with the general environment of the school, its strengths and its perceived weaknesses. They frequently became fascinated with the differing departmental cultures and, when they met beginning teachers from other schools, with the differing cultures of their respective schools.

(For one fascinating year, beginning teachers working in Hampstead worked with beginning teachers working in a local girls' selective independent school. The contrasts were sharp, but the beginning teachers found many more similarities, which surprised them as well as the teachers in the schools concerned.)

Although conventional readings and reading lists were given where appropriate, the constant aim was to get the beginning teachers both to read widely and to use their reading and their own experiences, to set themselves a personal research agenda. If items overlapped with another beginning teacher's concerns, joint work could be and was indeed undertaken. So central to the weekly sessions was the development of the beginning teacher's own research agenda.

During their actual teaching practice, the weekly seminars tried to deal with issues that had come up in the more informal conversations during the intervening week. The school-based tutor and the Institute of Education tutor had drawn up the programme of weekly sessions with this in mind. Although the order was sometimes changed, it was a pleasant surprise to find that we had usually chosen topics that met most but obviously not all, the concerns expressed. The focus was always to try to get the beginning teachers to ask the why and how type of questions, which would be firmed up in the school-based Enquiry, a research topic grounded firmly in school practice and undertaken towards the end of the first term and the beginning of the second.

These school-based Enquiries were generally undertaken with great enthusiasm and produced work of a high quality, despite being started during teaching practice and researched and written when the course was making extreme demands on beginning teachers' time. The range of topics was even wider than with the Area Study and hardly any topic has been left unexplored over the last few years. Examples included research on truancy, the links between education, training and work, teacher appraisal, disruption and discipline, IT provision, support teaching, provision for talented school students, dyslexia, refugee education, sexism in the curriculum, effective schooling, anti-racist teaching, bilingual support and the educational needs of school students at risk. The list is selective but gives an idea of the wide range of topics covered. (It also gives the subjects as topics, when in fact the beginning teachers produced the titles as research questions).

In many cases, the work done by the beginning teachers followed conventional lines, in that there was a discussion of the issue under investigation, an account of how the relevant literature gave understanding to the topic and then a school-based case study of some sort, relating both to the literature and the initial research question. What was new to us was the quality of the school-based research. This was due partly to specific help being given on research methodology but mainly to the beginning teachers' familiarity with the site of their research, and the help that was given in generous quantity and quality by the staff of the school.

A further spin off from the work was that many of these research projects were detailed examinations of school practice undertaken by 'critical friends' of the school. Collectively, they gave a fascinating snapshot of certain crucial aspects of school life and in some cases were seen as significant documents in relation to developing school policy. For example, one beginning teacher's examination of IT provision across the curriculum was undertaken within the context of a school policy development in the same area. The research projects were seen as valuable by a range of significant others and not only a part of an assessment process. Sharing the findings in seminars was a further learning process for the other beginning teachers.

The research undertaken for the school-based Enquiry also helped to deepen the contributions the beginning teachers made to their weekly meetings. Feeling more confident in their own abilities as practising teachers as well as educational thinkers, the weekly meetings became more intense and focused. Beginning teachers were confident in researching a topic and presenting their findings back to the group. In addition, the weekly meetings were increasingly being led by either the beginning teachers or by a member of staff not in the mentoring/ tutorial team, rather than by the school-based or Institute of Education tutor.

This practice was extended as the course developed and it was increasingly recognised that the school had great depths of educational expertise, often in areas where the Institute of Education either had few people or where the Institute had yet to recognise a topic with a staffing appointment. An example of the first would be bilingual support work, where, although the Institute of Education has an international reputation, it rests on the work of a very small number of staff. Yet Hampstead had had to provide a high level of expertise in this area and beginning teachers were exposed to this expertise at an early stage in their weekly meetings. It was thus established as an issue for all beginning teachers, regardless of subject orientation, (a subject discussed in more detail in Chapter 6 above) and given enthusiastic support by the ESL teachers, despite the high levels of demand that many such teachers already faced.

As the year started to draw to an end, it was felt that beginning teachers should be offered a further way of researching a topic revealed by practice in the school. The awareness was growing that the school had not only a great research potential in terms of their own staff and the beginning teachers, but was itself a prime research site.

Towards the end of a PGCE year, beginning teachers have finished much of their formally assessed work, teaching practice is over and, hopefully, a first job has been obtained. In Hampstead, it was felt this time offered a good opportunity for the beginning teachers to do some detailed investigative work, free from the usual external pressures that a PGCE course engenders. More, in this case, it could lead to the final formal assessment essay that went with this particular piece of the school-based course. For a few years, the Institute of Education and school tutors from a range of Camden schools, including Hampstead, got together to offer a practical set of research-based courses on key issues. The issues were chosen by being of significance and interest to the schools and to the tutors. Not surprisingly, they had a distinct urban, inner city focus. Topics included refugee education, counselling issues, EAL, utilising community resources and differentiated learning. Again, the work was school focused and based, with the research and development element to the fore. The results were again impressive, partly for the reasons stated and partly because the tutors involved were deeply committed and on this occasion, riding one of their favourite educational 'hobby horses'.

Many did in fact develop into the formal assessment. Again, similar favourable factors were evident. The work was of high quality, it was varied, sometimes in most unexpected ways, it was research based and it had, in many instances, immediate practical applications. For example, work on eliciting the educational needs of refugees led to some valuable work on school induction, particularly in relation to mid-term admissions. For the beginning teachers, the course had, in many cases, ended on a high note with a real sense of having achieved something of value to their own professional development, the educational research community and to the school and its students.

The research cultures in the school came to appear more explicit as a result of this final exercise. The constant questioning, the basis for much good education and research, meant that the beginning teachers saw the school not only as a place where they learned their craft but as a site for valued educational research. Here, the issues and questions that they discussed in the staffroom, departmental offices and in tutorials and seminars in the Institute of Education could be subjected to the analysis that good research offers.

Four other supporting factors were also at work in the school's role in this ongoing research process. The first was the increase in the range of long-standing links between the school and the Institute of Education. Many of the teachers had Institute of Education qualifications (PGCE, Diplomas, MAs) and the partnership encouraged this, up to and including PhDs and hopefully, the new EdD. Secondly, secondary education in inner London is still comparatively small scale and intimate in its relationships, in a way which still surprises outsiders. This remains true despite the abolition of the Inner London Education Authority, being part of the continuing feeling of solidarity that Londoners have about their city. Subject solidarity remains high and in the main, optimistic: the same is true of the senior management of schools, particularly at the LEA level. Few schools have taken on Grant Maintained status, partly perhaps because of this.

Thirdly, the changes brought about by the 1988 and subsequent Education Acts have begun to bed down, with the school having in place a wide range of structures and practices that has enabled it to operate successfully in the current educational climate. Fourthly, and connected to all the other factors, Hampstead was (and remains) a successful comprehensive school, particularly if value added criteria were to be used. The mixture of school students offers a rich learning environment and sets a range of fascinating research and pedagogic challenges to both beginning teachers and their mentors.

This links to a final point, that of hierarchy and status and the role that they play in helping to ensure, or impede, the development of a research and learning climate amongst a school staff. There are siren voices who would claim that the major problem with education in inner city schools like Hampstead is that there is too much educational theory floating around, particularly during the initial education and training of teachers. By this they often mean, without realising it, too much theory of a type they dislike and not enough theory of a type that they do. At its most crass, supporters of this perspective argue that educational theory and educational research, particularly that which they label progressive, has little to offer the educative process. They have particular devils: mixed-ability teaching, left-wing teachers and so-called real books are three examples. They have particular angels: uniform, selection and corporal punishment. They argue that it has been known for ages (by whom and on what evidence being unclear) that what successful education needs is a return to the basics of a good education, namely quiet, ordered and well-disciplined classrooms and school students, ruled over by wise pedagogues, with a belief in and mastery of (and it is usually thus expressed) teacher-centred whole class teaching. Like many dangerous and erroneous ideas, it has elements of truth. It also implies that progressive pedagogy decries everything that traditionalists hold dear. Like similar simplistic responses to criminality, the reality is more complex. Who in teaching is really against quiet, ordered and well disciplined classrooms and school students? Who can be against the aim of having competent, subject skilled teachers in a comprehensive classroom? Who was ever against excellence and parental choice for all? The reality is that placing such questions at the head of the list of desirable aspects of schooling begs many questions as to the purpose and content of education and also leaves unresolved the most effective way of reaching that desired state.

Such a negative stance does little for the morale of many teachers in inner city schools like Hampstead. It implicitly deskills them and also argues that the concept of teachers as sophisticated experts in curriculum design and delivery is a nonsense. It lowers their status and undermines their ability to make significant contributions to the betterment of their professional practice, a betterment based on their and others' research activities. The stance also encourages the trend to more hierarchical professional relations in school, as it confuses desirable moves towards greater teacher efficiency and effectiveness with more questionable ones relating to greater control.

Given this broader context, one of the catalysts that has helped sustain and develop the argument about teachers as active researching practitioners, within schools like Hampstead, has been the presence of beginning teachers in the school following courses based on a more genuine partnership between school and training institution than was often previously the case. Such partnership-based courses ensure that beginning teachers, right from the start of their course, become engaged in the ongoing research dialogue that has always been a feature of such good schools. And the role of the Institute of Education staff becomes much more integrated with the realities faced by both beginning teachers and their teacher colleagues, to the benefit of all.

At its most effective, this has meant a complex and rewarding mix of skills. Experienced and skilful teachers, deeply involved in their own practice, share their experience with the beginning teachers based on a common set of observations, for example of a recent lesson taken by the teacher or by the beginning teacher, or of some pressing pastoral concern. Questions are asked, issues raised and research questions posed. So much is not new, though perhaps the intensity is greater than it used to be. What is new are the extra levels of involvement in the school-based element of the training process by subject mentors, by the school-based tutor and by the close involvement of Institute of Education staff. Before financial changes made this impossible, a point discussed later, this meant an unprecedented amount of focused time was given to an individual beginning teacher.

It also led to the beginning teachers, as well as all those working with them, exploring, discussing and researching issues that were common to all. Interestingly, this new focus had the advantage that it naturally moved beginning teachers away from a simple subject focused learning process to a broader conceptualisation of the schooling process.

It is evident that in addition to the obvious training that the beginning teachers received, the scheme produced a great deal of valuable research, undertaken by the beginning teachers as a result of the research/practice model adopted. Their work was usually interesting and frequently illuminating for all of us lucky enough to read it. The beginning teachers' findings about the issues that concerned them in the school, often had a beneficial impact on their own practice, as they would sometimes acknowledge or their mentors confirm. Equally importantly, the results were sometimes illuminating to the school staff. All-round learning was taking place. It needs to be re-emphasised here that the beginning teachers' work was only one of the catalysts that helped make the school a researching school. This supported and supportive research ethos is one that Hampstead has developed over the years. It makes a dramatic impact on beginning teachers who have trained in the school and is often the envy of newly qualified teachers who come to the school from other initial training courses. Most important of all, however, is the impact on the pupils.

A final caveat has to be put in place and that relates to resources. Working in this way and supporting an innovative and research rich school environment has major resource implications for a school that, like most others in London, is always desperate for basic resources. If we want our teachers to be well prepared for working in our inner city schools, it has to be faced that it cannot be done cheaply and it cannot divert a school from its prime task, the education of its students. In the long run, it makes both economic and educational sense to put resources into initial education and training, of the quality that the partnership between Hampstead and the Institute has provided. It also requires political vision from those who run the English educational system.

CHAPTER 9

BEGINNING TEACHERS IN DEPARTMENTS 1: MENTORING IN SCIENCE

Jonathan Bach

The subject mentor has a clear responsibility to steer and guide, to teach and nurture the specific skills and competences which the beginning teacher needs to develop so as to perform successfully in the classroom. In addition the mentor must ultimately decide if these skills and competences are of sufficient standard to pass a PGCE or a BEd course The duality of role, as informal guide and first assessor, is distinctly different from the detached, supportive model of a mentor which is common in industry. It is even further away from Ulysses putting the care of his son into his old friend Mentor's hands three thousand years ago.

Beginning teachers of Science make specific demands on their mentors. Most schools expect a graduate scientist of whatever scientific discipline to be able to teach, with support, all the national curriculum areas of biology, chemistry, physics and earth science up to GCSE standard. However, this huge knowledge demand is usually beyond the majority of even recent graduates from relevant disciplines. Many degrees are very specialised and even topics in their so-called 'specialist area' may be bewildering to them: indeed, many science graduates have not studied one of the major sciences at 'A' level. Similarly, the mathematical demands of Science courses, even at GCSE level, can pose difficulties, Indeed, Ofsted have observed and noted mathematical errors in their observations of Science lessons.

Since there is a shortage of science teachers, schools continue to pursue mature entrants with experience in other fields. These teachers are extremely beneficial to a Science department but often lack or have forgotten many scientific concepts. Similarly, schools often expect beginning teachers to have excellent IT skills which they can pass on to other members of staff. This is also frequently lacking or there may be unfamiliarity in specific usage, for example, in relation to probes and data-logging in the classroom. Teacher training institutions can only begin to develop these skills in their beginning teachers.

All this means that the mentor must make sure that the beginning teacher acquires the knowledge, language and conceptual understanding required of a Science teacher and that continual updating, particularly of unfamiliar areas, is a continuing process. A willing and cooperative team of different subject specialists within a Science faculty, as we have in Hampstead, is an obvious benefit. Departments in other schools which are still subdivided into subject-areas therefore need to ensure such subject expertise is freely available to a beginning teacher.

Hampstead School Science faculty comprises 14 teaching staff and 3 technicians based in a self-contained building with 10 laboratories of various sizes and ages. In the turbulent 1990s, when the National Curriculum was being introduced, the department endured major building, staffing and curriculum changes. We feel that we have managed to maintain a stability which has enabled our incoming beginning teachers to join an enthusiastic faculty, in which the whole staff has supported their professional development. It is extremely important to us that beginning teachers join a welcoming department and that staff do not forget how challenging and exciting a new career is but also how frightening and intimidating a seemingly omniscient staff can be. Not only may it be a beginning teacher's first professional engagement, it may also be linked to a complete change of life style, such as new living accommodation and travelling requirements. Finally it involves the beginning teacher in building up professional relationships with more than 20 staff and upwards of 180 students. At Hampstead, as a result, the essence of mentoring is a slow development of the beginning teacher's role as a Science teacher supported by a developing professional relationship with a mentor.

The Induction Period

Mentoring is, of course, an integral part of the partnership arrangements between schools and HEIs. As an example of the development of partnership arrangements before the implementation of the current statutory arrangements, there was a joint scheme with the Institute of Education in London which took place during the first weeks of their preliminary school experience in October. We hosted a group of fourteen beginning teachers, among whom were two who came to us later on teaching practice. This preliminary experience consisted of a day a week for three weeks in the school, which provided an instant snap-shot of a functioning Science department and an overall impression of the teaching and learning strategies being used.

A brief tour and introduction to the school by year eight or nine students on the first day provided a school student's perspective of the school. Then the Head or a member of the senior executive team gave a brief talk on the school as part of the local community followed by the Head of Science, who talked about the structure of the department and its philosophy. However, for the bulk of the day, the beginning teachers observed Science lessons in groups of two or three. They were briefed in advance to focus on broad issues, such as classroom management, discipline, safe laboratory management, problem solving strategies and involvement of the students in the lessons. At the end of the day the Head of Department and Institute Science education tutor jointly debriefed the group and discussed any issues which arose.

The following week's focus was preparation for teaching. In small groups, the beginning teachers observed a lower school class and then discussed with the classroom teacher a specific activity, experiment or area of study that they could teach the following week. To make their input more akin to a real classroom situation, they were given a talk by the senior technician on ordering equipment and were then expected to order any equipment needed or to produce specific resources, with support from the classroom teacher. Their task was to lead a short portion of the lesson (approximately ten minutes), including some direct presentation to the students. Often two beginning teachers tackled different parts of the same lesson and this allowed peer review. The emphasis was not on producing a perfect part of a lesson but in having a go at teaching a class in a supported environment. This enabled beginning teachers to get over the fear and even terror of being in front of a class for the first time. They always knew that '*in extremis*' the classroom teacher would take over, although in practice this has never proved necessary.

The exercise was useful in allowing the beginning teachers some early 'hands on' experience and a chance to tackle the practicalities of teaching, as well as helping them to start evaluating their own practice and developing their own targets. In addition, classroom teachers other than the subject supervisor were involved from the outset in the early feedback on the lesson segment. The majority of the lesson segments were successful and inspired the beginning teachers with a degree of confidence in their ability to teach successfully in the future. Although a one-off activity, we tried to show how their lesson section fitted into a departmental scheme of work, within a five year programme for delivery of the National Curriculum, thereby touching on the planning of lessons early on.

Next, one of our recently qualified teachers talked to the beginning teachers about their first year as a Science teacher. The session took place with no tutors present, thus enabling a 'warts and all' viewpoint of the pressures and I hope, pleasures of Science teaching in an inner London comprehensive. Finally, at the end of this third and final day, a debriefing session focused on impressions and issues about Science in the school and on self-evaluations of the beginning teachers' lesson sections. We asked each beginning teacher to comment on the content of their lesson and the best and worst parts. Emphasising the positive parts encouraged discussion of successful strategies. In the discussions, broader issues also tended to be raised, ranging from school uniform and lunches to mixed ability teaching and assessment. These, we knew, would be taken up later in the course, either in the school or in the Institute.

We consider that after these three days of preliminary school experience, most beginning teachers have an idea about how a Science department operates; the planning, equipment and resources needed for every lesson; health and safety issues and the liaison with technical staff that practical Science teaching requires. Follow up and reinforcement is then made easy for us, when our own assigned beginning teachers return to the school later on in the term for the first teaching practice.

The first teaching practice

The number of beginning teachers in a department needs to be carefully considered, since timetabling with suitable classes and supportive classroom teachers may become difficult, even in a large department. More importantly, a mentor can only be effective with one or possibly two beginning teachers at a time. There are clear advantages and disadvantages for the beginning teacher to be paired up in a department. Mutual support and ways of adjusting to a school are counterbalanced by less time with the mentor and possibly being overshadowed by their colleague. On balance, we have come to accept that the advantages of peer support, when beginning teachers work in pairs, outweigh the disadvantages and we are able to make this possible in a large department such as Hampstead's.

The first teaching practice in our department, as in others in the school, will entail a gradual build-up in independent teaching. Initially, the beginning teacher will observe the classes s/he is going to teach and then begin part teaching and team teaching with the classroom teacher, eventually leading to the beginning teacher taking over the class. This gradual process is negotiated between the mentor, the beginning teacher and the classroom teacher and allows a steady increase in responsibility. Also, different classes can be taken on at different speeds. We need to challenge but not frighten a beginning teacher. A beginning teacher will be allocated about 40% of the lessons in a teaching week in their first practice and about 60% in their final practice. This still allows time for careful preparation and the chance to observe other Science teachers or to see the classes they teach in Science being taught other subjects. We are cautious and do not allocate beginning teachers to any year 11,12, or 13 classes but encourage them to team teach in their specialist area to broaden their experience with A Level or GNVQ teaching. We also attach a beginning teacher to a Science teacher's tutor group so that the essential but often neglected pastoral programme is sampled by the beginning teachers, for they are likely to be a tutor the following year when they enter a school as a newly qualified teacher.

At an early stage, it is vital that the mentor or Head of department makes clear the expectations of the department, its philosophy and standards and perhaps highlights relevant parts of the departmental handbook. We would rather state the obvious about time keeping, record keeping and participation in all aspects of departmental life than give the beginning teacher unclear messages. The beginning teacher is working in a demanding professional environment, with complex logistics and infrastructure, and they must adjust quickly to the specific environment – the busy school and Science department. A major part of a beginning teacher's learning comes through informal discussion or through listening to other Science staff at breaks, lunchtimes and after school. Most Science departments are geographically isolated and thus Science staff may be more insular than is true of many other subjects. However, this does allow a beginning teacher the opportunity to exchange information on crucial teaching issues and to develop the personal working relationships that greatly aid success in a school.

Linked to informal feedback, the mentor will need to make clear the expectations of a wide and possibly conflicting group of people involved in the beginning teacher's development. This is a difficult and important aspect of the role, as it can happen that the expectations of the university education department, the school department and the mentor can be different, particularly when trying to avoid needless duplication of lesson planning and evaluation notes, and marking and assessment policies.

Besides observing their own classes early on in their time in school, we also build in opportunities for them to observe all members of the department teaching. We view this as an important element in their training, as it allows them to see a diversity of strategies and teaching styles used by a range of teachers in different practical and experimental situations and with a variety of different age groups. It enables us to emphasise that there is no perfect Science lesson and that a teacher's individual style develops as a result of their personality and experience. The practical management of lessons can be likened to a form of art in its demanding nature; that is, teachers must ensure that meaningful results are collected by school students. It also means that successful manipulation of apparatus and chemicals often takes experience and possibly practical limits from the technical staff. For example, a discussion with the technical staff about a planned experiment involving acids and glass test tubes can be vital in ensuring safety. Beginning teachers often do not understand science class limitations when they are on their first teaching practice and we have a fundamental responsibility to ensure their and their pupils' safety in this regard.

When the mentor meets with the beginning teacher after they have observed others teach, there is a wealth of material to discuss from the individual lessons. It is easier from this practical basis to ensure that the beginning teacher becomes familiar with the department's and school's procedures and what may be their own esoteric methods for marking registers, monitoring absence, entering a laboratory and observing basic safety rules. Important policies, for example on safety, on language, and marking and National Curriculum assessments, can be drawn out of such a practice base.

It is clear then that we believe it important to allow the beginning teacher the time and space to become accustomed to the school, the department and the staff. The amount of time required for this induction process varies and is also constrained by the need for the beginning teacher to participate in lessons as early as possible. They also need to become involved with their potential classes within two weeks, even if it is only taking the register and supporting individual students with special needs in a class, if the teaching practice time is to be utilised to the full. The pattern at Hampstead is for the beginning teacher to gradually increase responsibility for both the planning (including ordering equipment) and delivery of the lesson, in consultation with the classroom teacher. Team teaching helps this process in that the beginning teacher is able to start building a relationship with the class, learn their names and any 'characters' and observe how an experienced teacher manages them.

The classroom teacher must appreciate that beginning teachers learn by their mistakes and these are a vital part of the learning process. It is often hard for the classroom teacher to stand back and watch a 'mistake' as they see it happen. The more that classroom teachers can let this happen before suggesting alternative strategies, the quicker the beginning teacher will learn that self evaluation is crucial. The ability to do this honestly is the most vital part of a beginning teacher's development. Many beginning teachers are at first undiscriminating about their performance. They may be too hard on themselves: not being able to pinpoint individual areas for development can make them depressed, as they only perceive that they are unable to deliver perfect lessons immediately and consistently. In contrast, the overconfident beginning teachers who believe they have nothing to learn, have proved much more difficult for the mentor. An honest self-critical approach from the outset is the best indicator of how much a beginning teacher will improve and develop over the year.

The Mentoring Session

The mentor needs to ask beginning teachers for *their* analysis of a lesson before embarking on their own comments, so as to build up their analytical skills by initiating a dialogue. Initially many minor points can be ignored, but beginning teachers should be aware of what they are not tackling. It is important to pick on a few, manageable, achievable targets. The mentor session is important for pin-pointing these, since, in an actively learning Science laboratory, it is easy to miss problems and minor disciplinary misdemeanours. It is even easier for beginning teachers to ignore and to miss things they should tackle but do not, for fear of confronting students. These issues need to be thoroughly dealt with from the outset by getting the beginning teachers to follow up incidents and advising them of the procedures to do so. For example, by checking they have done so, by observation, by discussion with classroom teachers and in discussion during the next mentor session. Although beginning teachers are initially nervous about being observed, it is crucial to build up a cycle of:

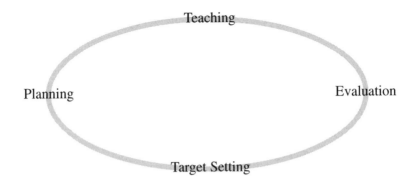

Teaching

Planning

Evaluation

Target Setting

The Role of the Classroom Teacher

Many Science departments have a teaching and learning policy or guidelines for classroom teaching. In addition to this, the mentor needs to give every teacher whose class will be taken by a beginning teacher, clear guidelines about responsibilities to the beginning teacher, particularly emphasising that they are legally responsible for the class and all the inherent health and safety risks in the beginning teacher's practical work. The school's code of practice for beginning teachers makes it clear that there is a school policy across all departments. (c.f. Appendix 2 for details of the Code of Practice.) In Science it is vital, because of the safety implications, that the classroom teacher must be in an adjoining room or at the back of the teaching room or laboratory itself. Indeed, apart from the safety reasons, the beginning teacher needs to be supported. The classroom teacher has to strike a delicate balance in this respect between interference and allowing the beginning teachers to try things out for themselves. Science laboratories are potentially dangerous and safety must be paramount, even if it means stopping a beginning teacher's lesson. However, cooperative planning and debriefing minimise the risks.

The Science department has followed the whole school guidance and participated in and contributed to developing the code of practice in the school. We had already followed these principles prior to the new legislation on teacher training. The process we adopt throughout the school is based on careful and close monitoring, feedback, advice and target setting. Ideally, the classroom teacher gives the beginning teacher verbal feedback on most lessons and a written comment sheet in a standard format each week. These written feedbacks should be positive and structured, with clear teaching and learning strategies. As in the rest of the school, the mentor and classroom teachers focus on one aspect of the lesson for their written comments, which can be agreed with the beginning teacher in advance. These build up from classroom management issues to problem solving, practical organisation and ultimately differentiation, active learning and independent learning. The beginning teacher receives a copy of all written comments and discusses with the mentor her or his view of their progress. It is important that the beginning teacher is clear about the mentor's view. Target setting is vital and the process is minuted in the form of the log used by all departments in the school. The beginning teacher is able to monitor her or his progress through being reminded of these key areas for action. In this task, the mentor is supported with the regular lesson feedback from subject teachers.

Challenges

These procedures apart, beginning teachers often feel Science is an easy subject to teach, as school students are motivated and often engaged in practical investigative work that they enjoy. Whilst this is true, laboratory work is not the panacea many beginning teachers hope it will be. It is harder to control safely a group of twenty Year 9 students doing experimental work on the reactions of acids, than a larger group doing questions from a worksheet. Many Science lessons require explanations of practical work with clear safety guidelines. The beginning teacher must be able to stop a class immediately if there is a safety risk and impose safe working practice on students. Thus, practical work requires more careful lesson planning than more theoretical work. It often needs experiments to be tried out in advance and safety literature consulted. A further problem, common to practical work in other subjects, is that it can easily turn into the formula of 'recipe following', rather than a challenging investigation of a kind that stimulates students and improves their conceptual understanding. Beginning teachers need to ask their students what has been learnt from their practical work and, as they gain confidence, talk to them individually about their progress. To do this effectively, beginning teachers need to clarify their own ideas about the nature of science and their science educational philosophy, which may be very different from that of the mentor. They also need to learn that the best teachers are facilitators, who support students' learning. Finally, all this work should link with the more theoretical work they do with the university team of tutors.

The biggest challenge for us as mentors is the beginning teacher who is not progressing and is in danger of failing. This can be for a variety of reasons, ranging from personal problems to lack of commitment to a teaching career. After due help and support has been given, the mentor, in discussion with all the tutors concerned, both in school and in the higher education institution, needs to ensure that the beginning teacher is able and equipped for a teaching post, or decide that they should not complete the course. To do this, mentors need full support from their heads of faculty, line managers and senior management within the school, as well as the university tutor. The beginning teacher needs to be told about problems and given clear written feedback as soon as possible. There need to be clear targets for them to work on and support for them to achieve these targets and this needs to come from both the school and from the university. The mentor has to liaise between all the parties involved, to ensure that the extra support is given. The greatest difficulties occur where a beginning teacher does not accept the views of the mentor and other members of a department. This has occurred in our work with beginning teachers and we have employed a range of strategies, such as involving the school-based tutor (c.f. Chapter 3), who worked with the failing beginning teacher directly and was able to liaise closely between the mentor, the beginning teacher and the higher education institution. We even considered a change of mentor, which we eventually rejected. The process of discussion about change itself raised issues which were time-consuming and demanding, key issues in their own right.

Time is clearly an issue. Mentors are invariably crucial members of their department and time is at a premium. The weekly seventy minute period of mentor time eases the problem. It is, however, inevitably insufficient for many beginning teachers but does guarantee an undisturbed meeting, ideally away from the telephone and other disruptions.

The role of a mentor in Science education is complex and demanding and ideally will result in supporting the beginning teacher in the transition from a student of education into an enquiring, competent and enthusiastic member of a Science department. The rewards are also high. The beginning teachers give their enthusiasm and skills learnt in other contexts and when we have been successful together in training, we have some excellent newly qualified teachers Indeed, we have appointed several from among them. We consider this to be the best comment on our work.

CHAPTER 10

BEGINNING TEACHERS IN DEPARTMENTS 2: MENTORING IN MATHS

Margaret Tetley

Hampstead School Maths Department has been taken part in the initial teacher training of beginning teachers from the University of North London for the past five years. The course, a two-year BEd in Secondary Mathematics, is specifically aimed at mature beginning teachers who come with a wide variety of backgrounds and experiences. In these five years, we have participated fully in the changes that have taken place and now we are in full partnership with the University and responsible for the assessment of Block Teaching practices in both the first and second years of the course.

Maths teaching at Hampstead is delivered by a team of nine full-time teachers. All are involved with the beginning teachers except the newly qualified teachers. The students are taught in mixed-ability groups in Years 7 and 8 and in banded groups in Years 9, 10 and 11. Beginning teachers are not formally involved with A Level teaching but have observed lessons and found and explored courses.

Four beginning teachers join the department each year: Two arrive at the end of September and stay until December, on their final teaching practice. Two more beginning teachers arrive in the Spring Term for their first Block practice one, which lasts about five weeks. As a mentor I have one extra free period (70 minutes) a week The budget to manage the free period is controlled by the school-based tutor as described in Chapter 3.

One of my first tasks for the beginning teachers is to agree their timetable with the Head of Department, the school-based tutor and the university tutor. It is important that we do not 'over-use' teaching groups or teachers from year to year so this is centrally monitored by the school-based tutor.

The beginning teachers are timetabled for about 12 or 13 lessons a week (out of a total of 20 periods). We aim for a broad balance of age and ability groups and include a PSHE lesson. We also try to include an opportunity for the two beginning teachers to 'team teach'. Beginning teachers are also attached to tutor groups throughout their practice.

The BTs arrive for a two-day induction about a week before second teaching practice in September. In this time we aim to answer as many 'nitty-gritty' questions as possible, so that maximum use is made of actual practice time. The beginning teachers will have sessions with the Head of Department, their mentor and the school-based tutor and opportunities to meet the teachers and classes they will be working with. They will be given copies of the school and the department handbook and are expected to write a general description of the school for their teaching practice file. They leave armed with their timetable and schemes of work, to return after a week ready to begin.

In their second block practice, we expect students to take over classes after an initial observation period. The order and timing of the 'take over' is carefully discussed by the student, the mentor and the class teacher. Ideally, the beginning teacher will be responsible for all their groups after three or four weeks. This observation period is crucial and we stress the importance of planning what is to be observed and of reflecting on the process afterwards. Beginning teachers may focus on a small group at this stage and follow them through a few lessons, monitoring their progress and looking at their written work. They are also encouraged to learn names as this avoids many later problems. Planning units of work begins at this stage. Here class teachers help with the detailed work and lesson plans are seen and discussed before each lesson. This observation stage also gives beginning teachers experience of a variety of teaching styles, as they are working with five different teachers.

As mentor, I hold a weekly formal meeting with the two beginning teachers. Discussion points are agreed; they are given a record of each meeting, and any action points are noted. As both mentor and assessor, I introduce the need for evidence that competences are being met at an early stage. It is important to pick up any difficulties early on so that we can discuss this with the University and suggest appropriate strategies. Each class teacher will observe the beginning teacher three or four times during the teaching practice and will give them and the mentor written feedback. The Head of Department and mentor also see each beginning teacher at work and often the university tutor visits too, and gives feedback and advice. This sounds formal but, in fact, most feedback is continuous and informal. The beginning teachers share our workroom and constantly contribute to our discussions and debates.

Our weekly meetings change in emphasis and tone as the weeks progress. At first, the beginning teachers ask many questions about the way things work and need much advice on class management and lesson planning. Soon specific targets are being set each week, as a result of formal and informal feedback from teachers and tutors, and these are followed up in the next meeting. By the end of the practice the mentor evolves into an assessor and with the beginning teacher completes the paperwork, summarising progress made and setting targets for the next phase.

As well as Maths teaching, beginning teachers are also involved with a tutor group and attend registrations, assemblies and tutor periods. Their experience of school-wide issues is widened by attendance at department, year and staff meetings; parents' evenings and school productions. As part of their teaching file they write a profile of one of the school students they teach, which also involves a wider view of the school. As a mentor, I am able to arrange meetings with other members of staff and I especially encourage contacts with the Curriculum Support and the Bilingual Support departments,whose work in this regard has been described in Chapters 6 and 7.

My role as a mentor changes during the teaching practice. At first I am a source of information and advice; as time goes on I hope to be able to help the beginning teachers to reflect constructively on their experience in the classroom. Finally, I have an assessment role based on my observations and those of my colleagues. It is important to get the right balance for these various functions and to keep all in mind during meetings with the beginning teachers. I communicate any doubts I have about the suitability of a beginning teacher as quickly as possible to the University Tutor – so that we can discuss any remedial action together and also to alert them to the possibility of involving the external examiner. Fortunately I have not had to do this very often.

We aim to help our beginning teachers to become competent and confident teachers. We have found that those who are willing to take advice are the most successful. When this is coupled with the ability to reflect on a lesson, the good points as well as the areas that need improvements, then great progress can be made. We know that the next time the teachers in training will be in a school full-time will be in their first teaching post, the following September. We are conscious of the need to give them an adequate preparation for this first post. In this regard, mentoring can sometimes involve saying hard things and setting difficult targets, but we have high standards and expect that they will be reached. I am pleased to say that we have had excellent beginning teachers with us in the department, who are now well launched on their careers.

Our relationship with the university is described as 'full-partnership' and this is an apt definition. The university staff are always available and ready to come in to school and help, if the need arises. We have benefited from their experience and we have contributed to the course. For example, each year the Head of Department and myself have attended conferences and run a session for tutors. New ideas and resources are shared, planning and schemes of work discussed. We have both been involved with the modifications made to the course in the light of the government's guidelines (DFE, 1992) and I have attended meetings of the course board and the examinations board at the university. Mentors are given training on a regular basis and these sessions have proved very useful, as we try to standardise our practice across participating schools. These meetings are held with mentors for a Modern Languages course, so general aspects of mentoring are discussed before we work in subject specific groups.

The extra work involved in the training of beginning teachers in schools is to some extent compensated for by the benefits to the department. Through the university we have access to recent research findings and developments in Maths education. Tutors who have attended conferences share ideas and resources as they are published. Beginning teachers are often full of ideas and enthusiasm and this spills over to the department generally. If we are commenting on the practice and approach of a beginning teacher this inevitably leads us to reflect on our own practice and the rationale for it. Our beginning teachers have also provided the department with high quality display material, which has been a source of inspiration long after they have left. For example, a display of beautifully designed kites, hung from the ceiling of the Maths corridor, was produced by the class of a star beginning teacher, who has gone on to develop an extremely successful career. Several beginning teachers have set up extra-curricular mathematics activities in lunch hour sessions, which have generated much interest from our school students. Mathematical activities of all kinds were introduced – one beginning teacher aquired a vast collection of games from car-boot sales. A group of beginning teachers from the university ran some very fruitful sessions for some of our girls, when graphics calculators first became available.

In conclusion, full responsibility for the block practice has had its advantages but I feel it has only worked because of the strong links that we have with the university tutors and the consistent and coherent approach we have developed over the years, i.e. the school stresses what the university expects and the university stresses what the schools expect when the beginning teachers are being prepared for teaching practice.

One major issue remains: the work of a mentor is time-consuming. Problems which arise must be dealt with promptly and this sometimes leads to unscheduled, lengthy sessions after school. It can be difficult to juggle the time available to do justice to the beginning teachers and to the other demands of the department. Obviously I try to delegate any issues arising from a particular teaching group to the teacher of that group and to deal with the more general issues myself, but delegation can only go so far. I am the link between the beginning teachers and the other teachers in the department, and also between the department and the university tutors. Time then, remains a factor. However, it is a stimulating role and has generally been very rewarding.

SECTION THREE:
TRAINING IN ITS WIDER CONTEXT

CHAPTER 11

MENTOR TRAINING EXPERIENCES IN PARTNERSHIP

Cathy Pomphrey

Introduction

My experience of mentoring began with the introduction of the articled teachers' scheme in 1990, when I was teaching at Hampstead School. This scheme was one of the first to have an objective of initial teacher training in partnership: in this case the partners were the school, the Institute of Education and Camden LEA. At first the term 'mentor' felt like a fancy title, with a Latin origin to give it added gravitas, for a job that many of us felt we had been doing for years, namely supporting beginning teachers on teaching practice in our school. However, unlike previous beginning teachers we had supervised the Articled Teachers would be in school for the greater part of their training. Thus, a radical rethink of the structures and content of school-based work was immediately called for. As the scheme evolved, so did our perceptions of the mentoring role. One of the first and probably greatest challenges was the need to redefine our respective roles and responsibilities as well as to clarify communications between the training partners. At the start we were all making assumptions about each other which often proved to be superficial and partial and threatened the coherence of the training experience for the trainees. Mentor training provided the forum in which we began to unravel these issues. Chris Watkins gives a useful account of some of this work (Wilkin, 1992, Chapter 7). The articled teacher experience threw us in at the deep end of school-based training at Hampstead and helped us to face challenges and raise questions which paved the way for new structures and relationships in training beginning teachers on other initial teacher education and training courses. While the scheme itself was short-lived (it was found to be a costly model and was discontinued in the secondary phase in 1993), it was a vital preparation for future training experiences, not least in terms of evolving the new mentor role.

Since leaving Hampstead in 1992 I have been developing a new PGCE Modern Languages course at the University of North London, this time as a university tutor. An important role for me now is working with mentors from Modern Languages departments in a range of North London schools, including

Hampstead School. My own experiences as a mentor have been invaluable in developing the partnership between the University and the schools and school departments. As well as the PGCE Modern Languages, North London runs a two year B.Ed course in Mathematics (see Chapter 10), both courses having a common framework for mentor support, using mentor training as an important forum for professional dialogue between school-based and university-based trainers. What follows is an account of the evolution of this professional dialogue as experienced through mentor training.

Margaret Wilkin describes two distinct models of mentoring (Wilkin, 1992, pp.24-25). The first sees the mentor as subject specialist and the mentor role as articulating the practice and principles of teaching the subject, while the second describes a needs-analysis approach which emphasises counselling, inter-personal and management activities. The view of mentoring which we have evolved combines aspects of each of these. In the early days of mentor training, many partnership schemes concentrated on communicating and clarifying the structures for whole school participation in initial teacher training. Because at the University we were initially dealing with only two subject areas, our profes-sional dialogue has taken place largely at departmental level and often focused on specific curriculum issues, such as content, while at the same time aiming to develop the necessary interpersonal skills for the interactions and negotiations associated with the mentoring role. This had the advantage of enabling tutors to evolve partnership structures together with the teachers who were to work on a day-to-day classroom level with beginning teachers. It also gave us some common understanding in terms of background and content for our delibera-tions. In this account therefore I shall concentrate on mentor training for the Modern Languages course.

Relationships and communications

Our first priority in mentor training was to set up the partnership in terms of the relationships and communications between mentors and tutors. As Vee Harris writes

> Although it is institutions and schools who set up and administer the partnership schemes, it is the individual tutors, teachers and trainees who must make it work, since they are the key members of the partnership (Harris, 1993).

Thus a primary objective was to establish our credibility and mutual respect as equal professionals. Having just left school teaching myself, I knew that teachers have to be very quick thinking, practical people, good at applying structures and principles to authentic situations, but usually reluctant to reflect without a clear pragmatic goal. However, given a practical problem or an authentic case-study which they recognise, teachers' reflections are likely to be profound and wide-ranging. An immediate common concern was to provide a training experience for beginning teachers which was coherent, supportive and realistic. Thus in building the relationship between the training partners, we used the needs of beginning teachers and the construction of the new course to provide the content of our initial collaborative work, hoping that the dialogue thus generated would help us to build trust and mutual, professional respect.

A common experience among us in our own training as teachers was the confusion, and sometimes disillusion and frustration, caused by what were often perceived as conflicting messages being conveyed by university or college tutors and teachers in school. Many of our early mentor training sessions included attempts to acknowledge some of these mixed messages and make them explicit. We had all been in the business of pretending (sometimes to ourselves some-times, and certainly to the visiting university tutor) that we were in agreement with the latest methodology, when our practice was actually informed by a complex combination of theoretical principles, features of the school context and personal qualities of both teacher and school students. Partnership ITET has meant that we have to be much more open and explicit about features other than the theoretical principles which inform teaching practice.

Other tensions we had experienced as Modern Language specialists related to what often appeared to be contradictions between the 'education' and the 'subject application' components of pre-partnership initial teacher training. Thus a commitment by both partners to integrating these two aspects, which traditionally have often been treated separately in teacher training courses, grew with the developing course content and structures. In all our early collaborative work, integration and coherence were key objectives.

We found that one successful way to lay the foundations for a constructive tutor-mentor relationship was to collaborate on clearly-defined tasks which could be incorporated into the daily work of the training course, much like 'active learning' tasks in the school classroom. Out of the collaborative process emerged a professional dialogue such as we had not experienced in the past. An example of this kind of collaboration was the joint production of materials such as proformas for documentation of course activities (e.g. classroom observation by beginning teachers or written feedback sheets for use during block practice supervision). This collaborative production helped us to share ownership of the course in the early days of partnership training and the tangible outcomes were proof of our joint efforts. As well as these products, however, we found the processes of production raised numerous professional questions, many of which continue to challenge us.

Another early priority was to agree principles and procedures for working with those beginning teachers who were struggling. We considered a number of case studies from our own experiences and pooled ideas for suitable support strategies, identifying the appropriate roles and contributions of both tutors and mentors in the process. Our discussions tended to start with class-management issues, but it was interesting to find that we could not separate class-management from MFL teaching and learning, a principle which has been concordant with the PGCE course's approach. For tutors it was invaluable to get a realistic sense of the everyday experience of beginning teachers when in school and the complexity of issues which need to be balanced when making what is often a spontaneous judgement in the classroom. This has enabled us to take a pragmatic and holistic approach in all our school and university-based work, so that we integrate issues such as equal opportunities, differentiation and class-management and organisation into our treatment of topics concerned more specifically with language-teaching and learning. Mentors, on the other hand, have an opportunity to step outside the context of their own school setting. They can review some of their spontaneous classroom responses in the light of the experiences of colleagues in other schools and gain other perspectives from tutors' knowledge of a range of school contexts, as well as theoretical insights derived from research. We found that by starting with a practical question based on an authentic case study, such as 'What would you say to a beginning teacher who produced a lesson plan like this?', we quickly raised a huge number of complex questions and uncovered all kinds of assumptions we were making about each other as training partners.

Articulating practice

These initial mentor training sessions helped us to build the partnership team and set up the new course. The role of the mentor we were assuming at this stage was largely one of support for the beginning teacher. It quickly became clear that this was not adequate and that mentors had to assume a training as well as a supporting role when beginning teachers were in their schools. Our mentors were skilled classroom teachers, but not necessarily equipped to articulate their good practice to beginning teachers. In pre-partnership days this was less important; the assumption was that after some observation of experienced teachers, trainees would then be able to practise for themselves if they were going to be any good at teaching. An important function of mentor training became helping mentors to articulate their classroom practice and develop 'lines' to use when talking about good practice with beginning teachers. The strategies we used to do this were again derived from good active-learning techniques, namely the use of role-play and authentic case studies. We looked, for example, at lesson plans produced by beginning teachers and compared a strong plan with a weaker one. This enabled us to raise the question 'What is good MFL teaching practice?'. We found that we could agree some general principles while at the same time accepting that there will be different, some-times conflicting practices advocated according to teachers' differing experiences, personalities and school contexts. By making these differences explicit we were able to articulate justifications for good practices, while reveal-ing shortcomings in some practice in a professional, non-threatening way. The theme of learning to articulate one's practice enabled mentors to share good practice: one memorable session took place in a school where a mentor tried this out by demonstrating to us developments in her department's use of IT in the languages classroom.

The theme of articulating practice also brought out some important differences in tutor and mentor perspectives. University tutors are often approaching practice via a critical evaluation from a more theoretical basis. This can make them seem over-simplistic or unquestioning to an academic. Our joint deliberations in mentor training have helped both sides. Through articulating their practice, teachers have realised the skills and knowledge they possess which has often been undervalued in the past. However, by breaking down the processes of acquiring such skills and knowledge, they have also come to realise the complexity of the activity of teaching and the need to evaluate and question, as well as proscribe practice. Tutors, on the other hand, have realised that an over-conscious application of theory to practice can inhibit the development of practical skills in the early stages of a training course. Critical awareness which follows some experience of practice is likely to be internalised better by beginning teachers and to inform their future practice and autonomy as teachers.

In the current climate of Ofsted and public accountability teachers can often feel threatened by the prospect of discussing their own practice too openly. This could be a result of past experiences of being criticised by tutors during their training and worrying that their practice does not coincide purely enough with the latest theory. This is particularly true of Modern Language teaching, where past methodologies have often been dictated by an over-literal application of a theory, such as the audiolingual methods which derived from behaviourist-psychology theories. Fortunately the communicative approach favoured in the National Curriculum is less dogmatically related to specific, unapplied theory. Our collaborative efforts to articulate practice and its related justification, both in terms of research and theories, as well as other considerations related to the teacher, learners and school context, have helped both teachers and tutors to review the practice and theory relationship, to the benefit of each.

The evaluator role

In the days before formal partnership in initial teacher training, the teacher's role in the evaluation and assessment of beginning teachers was minimal. Thus a good deal of preparation is needed for this aspect of the mentor's role which is much more extensive with partnership training. Two aspects of the role are particularly challenging for mentors. The first is the whole business of making appropriate judgements about the developing teacher's practice. Although most teachers in our partnership had an understanding and experience of formative profiling from school profiles and records of achievement, applying this knowledge and experience to commenting on another adult's teaching skill was demanding. After the first year of the PGCE course, we realised that the tensions between the supportive and evaluative roles were difficult for beginning teachers as well as for us. We decided that it was important for mentors (as well as tutors) to be explicit about this dual role from the start; after all we had a responsibility to professional standards as well as to individual development. In this way, as the PGCE year progresses and beginning teachers' confidence and experience grows, the evaluative role can become more prominent without beginning teachers feeling that support is being withdrawn or that they are being criticised in a negative way when evaluative comments are made. To help with this we agreed on procedures for feeding back lesson observations to beginning teachers to be used by the mentors and tutors who observed their teaching. The list of procedures for appropriate feedback was constructed collaboratively during a mentor training session and included the following advice:

- feedback should be interactive so that the beginning teacher's impression is heard and incorporated

- comments should be clearly related to descriptions of classroom activity and not simply judgemental

- pairs of beginning teachers in the same department should receive separate feedback differentiated to meet individual needs

- constructive feedback contains positive acknowledgement of achievements as well as short-term development targets

- weaknesses which could lead to failure of teaching practice should be identified as early as possible and the consequences made clear

- continuity and consistency between mentor and tutor evaluations should be aimed at and differences of opinion clarified.

One of the biggest adjustments for mentors was taking responsibility for the summative assessment of beginning teachers' practice. Most Modern Languages teachers were not even experienced in examining GCSE coursework, so for them summative assessment tended to be something others (such as Examination Boards) did. This responsibility therefore was particularly challenging for them as it implied an awareness of standards beyond those of the individual school or departmental context and needed thoughtful preparation. At first teachers felt unqualified to make such judgements and felt intimidated by the list of competences. Comments such as 'I can't even do all that myself' were not uncommon when faced with the DFE Circular 9/92 Competence List. Our team addressed this again by a collaborative production, this time of grade descriptions which identify a 'bottom line' for the passing of teaching practice and provide joint interpretations of the competence list in terms of realistic evidence to support judgements. These were subsequently written up for mentors and tutors to use as guidance when assessing. The process of doing this involved us in some stimulating professional debates about our expectations of newly qualified teachers.

Another important challenge associated with assessment and profiling is how to deliver the bad news to the weak or failing beginning teacher. This involves counselling skills beyond the merely supportive. However, mentors found that the work done to clarify and interpret the competence list made it easier for them to be confident in their judgements and clearer in their justification of assessment decisions. It also aided the identification of weakness at an earlier stage before it became entrenched. Mentors seemed reassured to have their judgements confirmed by tutors whose overview of a range of contexts in partnership schools and from contacts at a national level provided an invaluable yardstick.

As a result of their profiling and assessment of beginning teachers, many mentors said they felt better equipped to judge practice in their own departments and assess INSET and departmental development needs. They had also learned some strategies and lines for approaching the delivery of negative evaluations of practice in a constructive way. This they saw as useful experience for the role of 'critical friend' to colleagues in pre-Ofsted preparations and appraisal activities. We were all also less afraid to admit our own shortcomings in a climate where needs were discussed in such a constructive way.

Supporting further professional development

Furlong and Maynard (1995) describe a further role for the mentor, which is a step beyond the supportive or evaluative roles described earlier, and one which bears more equal status between mentor and beginning teacher than either of the former roles. They call this role the 'co-enquirer' and describe it as one of sharing the beginning teacher's more advanced classroom investigations as an equal researcher into questions about teaching and learning. Preparation for this role calls for support from the experience and research skills of the university tutor. The mentor (and tutor) role at this stage is one of challenge and encouragement of more ambitious undertakings as well as raising awareness of the subtleties and complexities of teaching and learning. In our discussions we became aware of our own frequent complacency once beginning teachers had attained a stage where they could cope satisfactorily with teaching and managing classes and we are currently investigating ways of approaching the role of 'challenger', so that more of our beginning teachers move beyond the plateau of 'good enough' teaching. We have found it is much easier to give directives and pass on strategies than to stimulate the necessary autonomous reflection and ambition involved in moving beyond the basic competence. However, without this challenge there is a danger of complacency and arrested development. To prevent this, mentors and tutors need to challenge the beginning teacher to refine his or her skills and develop a more critical awareness of the effects of teaching on learning and on learners' progress. This requires reference to theory and research and paves the way for more autonomous teacher development.

This stage of beginning teacher development has been our most recent preoccupation in mentor training sessions and mentors have been more than happy to address the more theoretical concerns it entails. Thus, in our mentor training programme we have progressed from collaborative tasks to sharing practice and developing skills and thence to reflection of a more theoretical nature. This has inevitably led to the contemplation of progressively more probing and detailed questions about the whole activity of teaching and teacher development. As we continue to reflect, a clearer picture of beginning teacher development over the training year is emerging and of the different levels of mentoring and tutoring needed, progressing from giving directives and strategies to suggesting options and negotiating targets, to encouraging enquiry and independent critical evaluation. The dialogue between mentors and tutors in the partnership is now reaching a stage where we are interested in evaluating and researching our own practice as trainers and we plan to include analysis of recorded feedback interviews by tutors and mentors in future mentor training sessions. The climate of trust and mutual support we feel we have achieved makes this a realistic development in our professional dialogue.

Another objective for the future is to support the spread of good mentoring practice to other members of the departments with whom we collaborate, so that the benefits of partnership are felt more widely than at present. Like most other partnerships, we now have a team of mentors who have joined us at different points in the programme and the developing, open-ended and interactive nature of the mentor training programme means that this is workable. The documentation we have developed as the dialogue progresses means that it is possible to fill in newcomers on the story so far.

In the North London partnership, as in many others, there is a great deal more overlap in tutor and mentor roles than has traditionally been the case. However, each partner also has a distinct role. Mentors still tend to look to university tutors for a view across the whole scheme, to ensure that relevant practice and issues are communicated from one school to another and that national trends and developments in teacher training are tracked. Mentors are becoming increasingly interested in wider issues concerning teacher training and MFL teaching. University tutors are able to maintain a realistic understanding of the local inner city context in schools and the effects of, for example, new arrivals in school who are refugees, on the role and practice of the teacher. Our experiences have led us to question the old theory and practice boundaries. We are optimistic that the evolution of our professional dialogue to a point where we are looking together at research questions coincides with a growing national interest in developing classroom-based research. We are already familiar with each other's strengths and constraints and we are in a much better position to work collaboratively on classroom research, which can have an immediate effect on practice. Our partnership work seems to have increased the interest and the confidence of local schools in the University's INSET and accreditation provision, now that they have some direct experience of how research and theory can help develop classroom practice. Mentors are more interested in further study than they were initially and we are about to embark upon a new accredited mentor training scheme.

We have come a long way since the days of the articled teacher scheme and the struggles to redefine our relationships and roles have been considerable. However the benefits of a flexible, evolving partnership between school and university are undeniable and open up some exciting challenges for the teaching profession.

CHAPTER 12

THE SUPPORT AND DEVELOPMENT OF NEW TEACHERS: A FIVE YEAR STUDY

Leon Gore

> The need to develop support systems for beginning teachers is a matter both of humanity... and teacher quality (Fullan, 1992, p.303).

My association with Hampstead School began in 1991, when I was appointed Camden's Initial Training and Induction Coordinator. In this role I have been welcomed into school to observe the teaching of newly qualified teachers (NQTs) and to discuss school-based and central induction. I have worked closely since 1991 with the Hampstead staff responsible for supporting and training the school's newly qualified and beginning teachers. Further, as co-tutor on the University of London Institute of Education and Camden Teacher Tutor Course, I was grateful to the many Hampstead staff who led sessions and regularly gave up time to participate.

When asked to write an 'overview' of recent teacher training developments in Hampstead School, I hesitated over the content. So rapid has been the pace of change affecting schools, higher education institutions (HEIs) and local education authorities (LEAs) that it is easy to forget where we were in teacher training at the beginning of the 1990s. I thought it useful, therefore, to trace these changes, focusing mainly on their effect on the induction of newly qualified teachers: it is impossible to avoid reference to initial teacher training since part of the government's recent strategy has been to develop strong links between them. I will also describe developments in induction in Camden in the light of the changes nationally and examine the factors that have influenced change.

Where were we?

An American research report on beginning teachers early in the 1980s concluded that nearly all teachers experienced great difficulties in the transition between initial training and the early years of teaching, where they had to cope on their own, (McDonald and Elias, 1960, cited in Fullan, 1992. See p.301-314 for a discussion of some of the American research findings on induction). Since then, the pressures on teachers have become more demanding and complex. Perhaps the greatest change has been how soon new teachers have to cope with the demands of the job. Managing pupil behaviour, working with parents, assessing pupils, meeting the needs of a wide range of ability, responding to linguistic and cultural diversity are just some of the complex difficulties with which new teachers have so quickly to become expert. For primary teachers the difficulties are compounded by the need to have expertise in teaching subjects as diverse as History, Design and Technology and Physical Education.

Successive HMI reports and the 1993 Ofsted survey on new teachers in their first teaching post have referred to the transition from teacher training to induction as the weakest link in teacher development (DES, 1988; DES, 1992; Ofsted, 1993a). The 1987 HMI survey on newly qualified teachers (NQTs) in England and Wales found 50% of NQTs visited had received less than adequate support from their schools (DES, 1988). A further survey based on visits to 42 LEAs revealed less than satisfactory or poor induction practice in a third of LEAs and 112 of the schools visited between 1988 and 1990. The Chief Inspector for Schools commented in his Annual Report for 1989-90 that there was often no link between LEA and school programmes, that the needs of new teachers were unclear and that induction failed as a bridge between initial teacher education and training (ITET) and teaching itself. The report also stated that clearer, agreed statements of the competences new teachers were expected to achieve would help to improve the transition. In the years that followed, this was a constant theme in the approach to the improvement of induction arrangements. (DES, 1991)

Matters were not helped by confusion over responsibility for induction following the 1988 Education Reform Act. Whereas in 1988 most LEAs accepted responsibility for providing induction programmes, the influence of the 1988 Education Act, with its changes in the management of schools, meant that by the end of 1990 there was far greater variation in perceptions of responsibility for induction. Some LEAs saw their schools as substantially responsible for induction. Under the 1990 DES Administrative Memorandum (DES, 1990), LEAs had formal responsibility for probation in LEA schools, but after the probationary year was abolished, the responsibility for induction rested with headteachers, though LEAs began to receive some funds to support the developments of initiatives in induction.

Themes and Strategies

The early 1990s can be seen as a time when serious attempts were made to deal with these repeated criticisms of the transition period. A major strategy of the then DES was the use of the system of Grants for Education Support and Training (GEST). The government sought to 'pump-prime' the development of good induction practice and induction training for NQTs became a new GEST activity for the financial year 1992-93. Financial support of two and a half million pounds, eventually divided over 43 LEAs in England, was to be provided for 'new and imaginative initiatives' to improve the link between ITET and induction practice (DES, 1991). LEAs were invited to make competitive bids showing how their new induction activities would alter or enhance their present induction arrangements.

All of the LEAs making bids received some funding for induction for the years 1993-95. The overall squeeze in LEA funds meant that LEAs became reliant on this GEST provision, which varied year by year, for funding central induction programmes and for supporting school-based induction work. Until 1994-95 LEAs were allowed to manage the induction funds centrally, but for 1995-96 LEAs had to provide a formula for the devolvement of all GEST induction funds to schools. For 1996-97, induction disappears as a separate GEST category and is included as a necessary, but inevitably competing area for expenditure within the grant for the category called School Effectiveness. These frequent changes, as well as uncertainty about funding provision, have not helped us to establish and sustain good induction practice.

The guidance for eligible expenditure given to the LEAs for GEST bids for 1992-93 was divided into six areas. Mentor/teacher-tutor training was one area. However, apart from the induction arrangements for EU teachers, only one of the other four areas represented a significant departure from previous LEA practice. This referred to joint activity with initial teacher-training institutions, giving as an example the development of profiling and competence-based approaches for the assessment of beginning teachers.

Various LEAs began producing New Teacher Competency profiles (e.g. Essex, Cleveland, and Surrey LEA with the Roehampton Institute of Education). At the same time the Northern Ireland Initial Teacher Training Working Party, the Open University and also the DFE were each constructing competence profiles for beginning teachers. The Northern Ireland Working Party went further than others and anticipated later initiatives from the Teacher Training Agency in its attempt to frame a career-long profile, with different competences emphasised at the three phases of ITET, induction and INSET.

The involvement of institutions of higher education (HEIs) in induction and the development of a competence-based career entry profile have since 1992 been two constant themes in the government's approach to induction. Paradoxically, almost at the same time as there has been the move to involve ITET institutions in induction, there has been a determination to shift the responsibility of the initial training of teachers from HEIs to schools (c.f. DFE, 1993b), One consequence and perhaps one of the most positive outcomes of the new ITET partnerships between HEIs and schools has been the professionalisation of schools' staff involvement in teacher training.

The argument that involving schools far more in initial teacher training supports the transition of beginning teachers to full school life and is also helpful towards making productive links between schools and HEI, appears entirely reasonable. However, such arguments need to be seen within the wider context of government policy. First, it has been part of government education policy to weaken the power of LEAs and the approach to induction has been consistent with this. Three years of encouraging LEAs to develop good induction practice in their schools was followed in September 1995 by the devolvement of all LEA induction funds to schools. This has made the survival of LEA staff concerned with providing induction problematic. There is a danger that enforcing a market approach to induction will result in less support for schools, erratic provision and the undermining of advances made in previous years.

Second, the early 1990s saw government attempts to assert increasing control over the structure and content of initial teacher training courses. Most evident examples are the insistence on and specification of the amount of time that beginning teachers need to spend in school. Circulars 9/92, 35/92 (DFE 1992 and DFE 1993b) set out new criteria for courses, with consequent funding arrangements for the initial training of teachers and stipulate the teacher competences required for qualified teacher status for each phase. The introduction of the competences can also be seen as part of the government's attempt to find a way of measuring teacher training outcomes and effectiveness and as part of what it would no doubt describe as a more rigorous approach to accountability in education in general.

Induction in Camden

In 1990, when Camden became an LEA following the abolition of the ILEA, the national picture, one of great variation in induction practice, was only partly reflected in its schools. The ILEA had introduced induction support for NQTs in the late 1970s and many of the good induction practices of the ILEA remained. Schools in the main believed in the importance of providing a lighter timetable for NQTs and in enabling them to attend the central provision, made up of half-day subject specialist and general induction sessions. Within Camden Education Department there was also widespread sympathy for resourcing induction for NQTs, which before cuts in local authority spending was translated into support for NQTs by continuing the ILEA's practice of financial support to schools for the release of NQTs to attend LEA central training and school-based training. INSET and central support for teacher tutors was also funded.

However, there was little evidence in practice of a consensus across Camden schools of the aims of a school-based induction programme, nor of what NQTs should be achieving during their induction year and what constituted appropriate levels of support. There were differences too about the role of the NQT's teacher-tutor and tension over the part played by the teacher-tutor in the formal assessment of the NQT. The variation in the status given to this role in schools reflected the lack of common understanding. In secondary schools, with rare exceptions, the responsibility lay in the hands of a member of the senior management team and supporting NQTs had to compete with many other priorities, at a time of great educational change.

The belief in the importance of induction in Camden went beyond a recognition of its attraction to prospective NQTs at a time when authorities were competing to recruit and retain teachers. The welcoming letter from the Director of Education to NQTs stressed the importance of teachers reflecting on their own experience and sharing their thoughts with their colleagues. There was a strong belief that professional development must be good and must work, if sometimes indirectly, to pupils' benefit. Critically, too, a valuable induction experience was one process through which Camden was able to convey what it expected of its teachers and schools and what they should expect of Camden's Education Department. The induction experience is one element in the development and transmission of the ethos and cultural identity of Camden LEA. This identity has been one in which a commitment to the achievement of all pupils has been seen as fundamental. 'Teachers should provide a demanding learning environment and a programme of learning which enables students from all backgrounds and of all abilities to achieve their full potential'. (CLEA, 1991b, quoted in all Camden induction folders from 1991-1994).

Camden has also conveyed its expectations to NQTs through the involvement of its inspectorate. At the beginning of the 1990s the Camden Inspectorate's visits to both primary and secondary NQTs revealed marked differences in schools' attention to various aspects of NQT induction. Particularly, NQTs needed to understand that by planning for all children's needs and by keeping a detailed teacher's file, they would raise achievement in their classes. By coordination between schools, the inspectorate and the induction coordinator, attempts were made to ensure greater consistency across the LEA, in schools' expectations of NQT planning and record keeping. Induction was also seen as important in encouraging positive attitudes to professional development among Camden's teachers. Camden has continued to believe that the quality of its education depends on teachers 'who feel supported in the process of continuous learning and development for themselves and their pupils' (CLEA 1991b). Accreditation was one strategy Camden adopted to encourage NQT's to sustain an active commitment to their professional development.

The Professionalisation of Induction and the involvement of HEI

Camden had anticipated government moves to involve HEIs in induction for newly qualified teachers by collaborating with the London University Institute of Education (ULIE) to create an induction programme for NQTs that would enable them to submit work for a third of the new Academic Diploma in Professional Studies. The appointment of Camden's Initial Training and Induction Co-ordinator was made jointly with ULIE and was partly funded by ULIE for three years. As part of this initiative Camden was prepared to register all primary NQTs for the new Academic Diploma.

ULIE also made available time for staff to support Camden's induction coordinator in developing a programme to enable NQTs, to submit work for the Academic Diploma. Initially introduced for primary NQTs, accredited induction met great hostility from NQTs and schools, who perceived it as yet another imposition on NQTs in what was usually the most difficult year of teaching, rather than as an opportunity. Primary teacher-tutors saw accreditation as a distraction in the support of NQTs and argued that an accredited programme would have been more appropriate for experienced teachers. So, measured by NQTs going on to complete submissions, this initiative was conspicuous by its lack of success. Yet, the strategy may have had incidental success in the seeds it sowed. It reinforced the message that the authority was prepared to direct resources to professional development, that teacher development needed to be approached in a more systematic way than had often been the case and that extra non-contact time was not sufficient for NQTs because there also needed to be some analysis of their needs and some planning to meet these needs.

Other influences emerged from Camden's close relationship with ULIE. Government changes in initial teacher education meant that BTs would have to spend far more time in schools than previously. This would change the relationship between HEIs and schools and new partnerships would need to be forged. ULIE had recently been in partnership with Camden and four of its secondary schools, including Hampstead, in the articled teacher scheme which had involved schools taking on major responsibilities for the training of teachers, over a two year period. The partnership experience of the articled teacher scheme was significant in easing the transition to school-based initial teacher training within secondary schools in Camden. This was mentioned in the previous chapter, which also stated that the ULIE secondary articled teacher scheme explored the critical role of the mentor, the link and co-ordinating tutor within the schools (see Watkins, 1992). An evaluation of the scheme based on interviews with the mentors pointed to the clear benefit of the professional development of the mentors' expertise and confidence as teacher trainers (CLEA, 1993). The concept of the 'mentoring school', emerged and with the area-based scheme the mentor role evolved and became formalised into that of link tutor.

The articled teacher scheme raised thorny issues on the assessment of teachers, and led schools like Hampstead to accept the responsibility for failing beginning teachers (initially, an aspect of the partnership in which there was a lack of clarity). The increased role of schools in the teacher training partnership also gave impetus to schools and ULIE to establish consistency of aims, not only within and between schools and ULIE, but just as importantly, across Camden schools. In the early stages school link tutors, ULIE tutors, LEA representatives, worked together on programmes and training. This gave opportunities for sharing strategies and helped to give meaning to the notion of 'partnership' between the Camden schools as well as between schools and ULIE.

The 'professionalising' of teacher support for beginning teachers, the serious thought given by secondary schools such as Hampstead to the respective roles of heads of department and heads of year in initial teacher training has had an impact on the induction provision for secondary NQTs.

At this point, however, it is worth sounding a warning note. Research into an experimental school-based primary teacher training course reported by Dr Jill Collison at the British Educational Research Association conference in Oxford 1994 found that mentors 'essentially ignored' the beginning teachers. The mentors, though, believed that they were supportive of the trainees and involved in their training at a level that went beyond teaching practice supervision. Collison argued that the nature of primary school classrooms militated against effective mentoring and that the lack of non-contact time was a real problem and that most teachers had not yet made the necessary leap in understanding of their new role (Collison, 1994).

Secondary schools do appear to lend themselves more easily to the reforms in initial teacher training, but they too are very busy places and time for supporting beginning teachers and NQTs is frequently an issue. Mentors also require support and a forum for reflecting on their roles, otherwise the argument that mentoring provides the opportunity for 'professional development' could be treated with cynicism by hard-pressed teachers. A school teacher training group such as has such as the one set up in Hampstead School is an exciting initiative for the support of mentors.

Guidelines and Straightjackets

To assess beginning teachers, subject departments in schools and HEIs needed to discuss and agree criteria and methods for determining progress. From the Institute of Education, its partner schools and Camden there emerged a notion that there had to be a helpful method of recording teachers' achievements, beyond the summative report at the end of teacher training and the formal completion of the probationary year. The terms professional development portfolio (PDP) and profile were frequently used – often interchangeably at first – and their meanings confused. The emphasis of the former was very much on self-reflection through beginning teachers sampling aspects of their work. Sampling pupils' work had become an acceptable method for teachers to assess and describe pupils' progress. There were benefits in teachers using the same approach for themselves. The PDP approach would give teachers ownership of the portfolio and the process of assessing their development, but its worth would depend on the teachers' ability and commitment to reflect honestly on their own practice.

The term *profile* became differentiated from the concept of a PDP and was used to refer to the written assessment, discussed with the BTs at the end of their training. It aimed to involve BTs in their own assessment and achievement and to be fairly comprehensive in its approach to the teachers' role. However, the introduction of the two government circulars (DFE, 1992 and DFE, 1993a) imposed a DFE notion of profiles which was narrowly competence-based. The competences required for qualified teacher status have been criticised for omitting the wider professional role of teachers and other aspects of teaching. In her critique of the 9/92 Circular, Thompson makes some important points. She states that the competence-based assessment implicit in the Circular divorced teacher performance from underpinning intellectual, cognitive and attitudinal dimensions (Thompson, 1992). Also implicit is the assumption that once competence has been achieved in one area, for example, subject application or classroom management, further development will not be needed. In addition there is the absence of a concept of teaching as exploratory, i.e. with teachers evaluating their own practice and problem solving. Also missing from the DFE competences is the notion of context. These competence statements are proposed in the same format whether the context is an inner urban school, with an extensive profile of social deprivation, large numbers of pupils on free school meals, poor housing, poor employment prospects, high staff turnover, strong anti-school peer culture, or whether the context is a selective grammar, where little of the above pertains and where there is a tradition of strong academic achievement and active parental support. (This subject is discussed more fully in the next chapter.)

The TTA has since built on the DFE competences and the profiles constructed by LEAs and HEIs to provide a career entry profile for teachers. Competences have been given a set of descriptors to guide assessment. An alternative set of descriptors is provided when beginning teachers demonstrate that they have a particular strength in a certain competence. The intention is that newly qualified teachers will be able to have their induction training and future professional development better targeted as a result of having this career entry profile. There are evident advantages in the existence of this common language, but common statements can become reified and divorced from experience and so it is important that these descriptors should remain as guidance and not become prescriptors.

Sustaining and developing a culture of induction support

Through all the discussions and developments in profiling, most of Camden's teacher tutors have been less than enthusiastic about a competence-based assessment. The model of teaching implicit in this approach caused concern. It was seen to conflict with views of teachers as reflective practitioners and life-long learners, developing their practice. As a result, Camden retained its own interim and end of year achievement and assessment reports, beyond the ending of the probationary year. These evolved through consultations between Camden Education Department and schools. The headings on the forms are broad and are presented to teacher tutors and headteachers as general areas for comment, rather than as specific competences. Camden wanted to encourage discretion in the use of discrete statements of competence, and wished to sustain holistic approaches to assessing NQTs. These reports continue to be written extremely conscientiously and provide rich descriptions of teachers' progress. They contain evidence of teacher tutors and heads of departments bringing their own experience to bear in analysing and making sense of the development they see.

Camden has tried to provide further support for NQT development. NQTs are encouraged to keep a structured professional portfolio. This portfolio represents a compromise between the PDP undertaken at the Institute of Education which aimed to develop teachers' self-reflections, and a modified form of the Surrey LEA and Roehampton Institute of Education's *New Teacher Competency Profile* (SES, 1993). The Surrey profile was trialled with a small group of NQTs in Camden and Camden has made use of certain aspects for its induction portfolio, following the suggestions and comments of the 1993-94 group of Camden NQTs and teacher-tutors.

The Camden portfolio given to NQTs contains an *aide-memoire* rather than a group of competences. This *aide-memoire*, while influenced to some extent by the Open University's teacher competence model (OU, 1994), borrows heavily from the work on the initial training of teachers by the Northern Ireland Working Party chaired by Geoff Whitty (Northern Ireland Working Group, 1992). This working party presented competences as aspects of the teachers' role which would be developed over a teaching career, with the emphasis on different aspects at different times, during initial training or induction or continued professional development. The Northern Ireland framework gave considerable attention to the wider role of the teacher, for example, the teacher's interaction with the school's community, and a teacher's contribution to the school debate about school development and improvement. The framework also included competences of reflection and evaluation.

The experience of a number of the LEAs which made up the old Inner London Education Authority has shown how quickly commitment to induction for NQTs can be dissipated and how LEAs need to work at finding the best means of supporting their schools to work with their NQTs. Hampstead was one of the first Camden secondary schools to formalise its thoughts on paper about good practice in induction for NQTs. A member of its staff led sessions on school-based induction programmes and presented documentation detailing the roles and expectations of departmental and pastoral heads in the support and development of NQTs in 1993 and 1994 for the Camden/ Barnet/ ULIE Teacher Tutor Course, which many teacher-tutors from Barnet and Camden attended. The second year of the course was made up mainly of Camden teacher-tutors and included many mentors from Hampstead School.

The course was one element in the attempt to develop a 'mentoring' culture in Camden. It explored the skills involved in mentoring, for example, the process of analysing needs and active listening. It addressed concerns about the observation of NQTs, the negotiation: the purpose; the how and what to observe; the role of the observer (participative? non-participative?); and even the seemingly mundane matter of entering and leaving the NQT's classroom. The course enabled teacher tutors to consider how to feed back in a constructive way that would manage to take NQTs forward. It examined target setting and feedback and importantly the setting of success criteria for those targets. Teachers felt very inexperienced in the whole process of observation and feedback. (At that time, 1993-94, hardly any of the teacher tutors/mentors had appraisal experience). Time was given to concerns about struggling NQTs and the difficulties this posed. Teacher-tutors explored their changing roles as they moved from the position of supportive friend to that of assessor, learning what was meant by the expression 'critical friend'. Teacher-tutors were involved in defining what it means to be 'professional', generally, as a teacher and specifically within the context of their schools, and explored what might be the attributes of a 'reflective practitioner'. Teacher-tutors also had the opportunity to reflect on what should be considered in assessing a teacher and what a written report should encompass.

Such a course, however, could only reach a small number of teacher-tutors and mentors and aspects have now also been introduced in annual teacher-tutor training sessions in Camden. Though a relatively small number of teacher-tutors and mentors attended the ULIE course, its significance also lay in the statement it made about the importance and status of the role of supporting NQTs. This message was underlined by Camden's participation in the NFER research into induction (c.f. Earley, 1992; Earley and Kinder, 1994) and the evaluation of other Camden induction provision by interviews with primary Camden NQTs carried out by ULIE in 1993, in response to Camden's request.

Expectations have also been clarified through the regular visits of the induction co-ordinator to schools. The visits have several functions for the induction co-ordinator:

- *support for NQTs* – to observe NQTs in ways of their own choosing without any assessment implications, to share perspectives, and for the induction co-ordinator to suggest developmental strategies

- *monitoring induction* – to obtain some individual feedback on the NQT's experiences of central and school-based induction provision

- *support for teacher-tutors* – to talk to teacher-tutors about their concerns and their own experiences of the role.

A 'mentoring culture' needs time to grow if it is to have more than a patchy effect within an LEA and its schools. Particularly in the primary sector, and increasingly in the secondary, many current Camden teacher-tutors and mentors were recent NQTs themselves. The attention given to their support is bearing fruit, in their willingness to take on the responsibilities of the teacher-tutor/ mentor role and in the quality of support they give their NQTs.

Other influences on NQT support and development

Other educational developments have also had an indirect influence on induction. The school effectiveness and school improvement research, which no school can ignore for long, has pointed to staff development as one feature in the development of a school's effectiveness. Widespread interest in this research and Ofsted inspections have stimulated schools to look more rigorously at pupils' progress and teaching and learning.

In concluding, I would like to strike one positive and one negative note. I have visited a good number of Camden primary and secondary NQT classrooms over the last five years, at a time when teaching has become increasingly demanding. My impression is that NQTs are better prepared to succeed in teaching than ever. This has not come about through any one cause but I would suggest that important factors have been: the contraction in other employment opportunities; the greater involvement of schools in initial training, which in turn has given an impetus to the teacher training departments and colleges to ensure that the part they play is effective, and the involvement of schools in the selection of candidates for initial teacher training and education.

However, since the abolition of the probationary year there is an increasing tendency for schools to employ NQTs on temporary contracts and this is of great concern. There is a danger that schools will give less time to managing the development of NQTs who are struggling and just replace the NQT at the end of the contract. Many NQTs who have very difficult first years go on to develop into fine teachers. Many potentially effective teachers will either not be given this opportunity or will reject teaching because of one unhappy experience.

CHAPTER 13

THE SCHOOL IN THE CITY
Crispin Jones

> To raise the level of urban education across the board will require money; but money is not enough. We will need teachers; but teachers are not enough. We will need research, and educational research is already giving us new teaching techniques, new methods of evaluating academic progress, and a host of additional aids in educating the slum child. But research is not enough. (Halt, quoted in Duckenfield, 1995, p.9)

Perhaps the word 'slum' gives the game away. In England we no longer talk about slums or slum school students. This is more about euphemisms than progress. Harold Halt, writing about American inner city schools in 1968 had fewer qualms. And it is to the United States that we should go to again, to see what happens if we abandon our inner city schools. Duckenfield, in his recent OECD study of urban schools, also quotes Jonathan Kozol, who, writing in 1991, observed

> Looking around some of these inner-city schools, where filth and disrepair were worse than anything I'd seen in 1964, I often wondered why we agree to let our children go to school in places where no politician, school board president, or business CEO would dream of working. (Ibid. p. 9)

Schools in inner London have, it is to be hoped, not deteriorated as much as those in some US inner city areas but the warning is there for us to heed. So is part of the remedy: as Halt says, good inner city schools need money, they need good teachers and they need good educational research. Most importantly, as Kozol notes, they need commitment, not just from those who attend and work in them but commitment from the wider society. If our inner city schools become decoupled from an uncaring wider society, the social consequences are likely to be dire. Hence the importance of training beginning teachers for work in such schools.

Much of the book so far has been concerned with the intimate detail of such working with beginning teachers in one, successful, inner city school. At this point, it seems important to describe this inner city context in more detail, highlighting some of the key issues that this context imposes upon education and teacher education in particular, and why the particular form of working with schools and beginning teachers described so far in this volume seems both effective and appropriate. In doing this, this section of the book examines how we might better understand urban areas and the schools within them more generally, in particular the diversity and composition of the communities that such schools serve and the consequences of this understanding for the training of teachers who will work in such schools. A further area, the effective school movement, which has the urban school as a major focus, is also briefly addressed, its value being seen as clear but perhaps more limited in scope than some of its more uncritical proponents accept. Finally, seen as more appropriately placed in an appendix to the main text of the book, there is a brief discussion of the role of HEIs in the training of teachers for the inner city (cf Appendix 3).

To start with, it is crucial to understand better the urban areas that we work in and prepare teachers for. The starting point for this has to be a clearer understanding of what exactly is this London that we prepare teachers for working in. This is because London, like many other large urban conglomerations like New York, Tokyo and Mexico City, no longer has clear boundaries and is a most complex human institution, difficult to understand and indeed, control. In administrative and legal terms, lines are drawn on maps to designate the London boroughs, which in turn combine to make a larger but less clearly defined administrative unit which we might call London. Then there is inner London, at one time being seen as coincident with the Inner London Education Authority (ILEA) but which excluded London boroughs like Newham and Waltham Forest, which had many of the educational features of the ILEA boroughs. To make matters more complex still, the traditional link between residence and workplace becomes more and more attenuated. People commute into London from all over the South East of England, so that the link between residence and responsibility is weakened. Inner city issues are left behind as the commuters move into what have sometimes been called the 'exurbs', residential areas and towns beyond the traditional suburbs, most, but not all, in the London boroughs.

London, however defined, has had no real government of its own since the abolition of the Greater London Council by Mrs. Thatcher's Conservative administration in the 1980s. Little strategic planning now takes place and certainly little is done within a London-wide framework with some form of local democratic accountability. In terms of education, this means that London now consists of a range of Local Education Authorities (LEAs), some Conservative, some Liberal Democrat, some Labour and some run by forms of alliance between these three parties. There is little overall educational planning across the city and school students living in adjoining streets with a borough boundary between them may well face very different educational offerings. In addition, parental choice cuts across these boundaries and recent changes in the governance and control of schools have meant that many LEAs now undertake little more than an educational 'sweeper' role. London-wide issues, such as Traveller education and meeting the educational needs of refugees have to be dealt with at a local level, often meaning inadequate services are available to help meet need such specialised needs.

Most beginning teachers who train in London have little knowledge of this state of affairs and of its antecedents at the beginning of their courses. Yet it is important for beginning teachers to gain some understanding of the historical and continuing development of cities in general and London in particular. The more they know about their school students, the more they will be able to understand them and their actions and, one hopes, the more they will be able to meet their educational needs. Such knowledge and understanding of urban systems (including schools), need to be placed in a conceptual framework, which is, in turn, mediated through the political perspectives that may be held by the beginning teacher and those who work with them during their training. That London's teachers and teacher trainers are all left-wing radicals is an urban and political myth. Teaching is inherently a conservative practice of passing on the best of the past, in a critical and informed manner, to future generations. (In passing, it is worth noting that few see the legal profession as revolutionary, yet its alumni contain most of the leaders of the French Revolution, such as Danton and Robespierre.) This myth of left-wing bias amongst teachers and teacher trainers links in with another myth, though this time one without a specific urban focus, that education can be made into a non-political activity. The education of the citizens of tomorrow could hardly be a more contentious and political issue, as current political debates around educational issues well demonstrate. Indeed, it is the range of opinion on current educational issues that makes the training process so challenging, as assumptions can seldom be slipped past a group of beginning teachers. And this broad political debate is particularly loud in relation to inner city schools. This is not so much because they are seen as failing, which of course many are not, but is more to do with the fact that it is an educational subject that can be argued over at an impersonal level, as few of the participants to the political debate send their own children to such schools. In addition, such debates, particularly if they are to be discussed by beginning teachers, need to be located in a range of firm intellectual understandings, not least of the complexity of London's urban history, for it is an understanding of that history that helps to give part of the answer to questions like 'Why are these children, at this time, in this city, in this part of the city, in this school?"

In terms of such a history, a key question would be why cities like London grow, decline, or indeed, do neither. Equally important would be questions as to what sort of growth is being talked about and the value that is being placed upon it. For example, the surface area of London continues to grow but its population continues to decline. But even those seemingly straightforward facts contain assumptions. The population of the London boroughs does indeed, in the main, continue to decline, but the London region's population is on the increase. Other criteria of growth could be growth in terms of *per capita* income, indices of production and consumption and so on. The point of this is that beginning teachers should be made aware of the illusory nature of sweeping statements about the areas that they are working in. Population decline appears to be a disaster but so was the dreadful overcrowding to be found in many parts of London (and of course in other major British cities) up until the Second World War.

The history of London is also a history of attempts to provide a mass education system for its young people. The 19th century debates about the purposes of mass education are still relevant today, as indeed are the debates about the professional preparation of teachers that took place at the same time (Grace, 1979). Fascinating questions also emerge from a contemporary contemplation of aspects of this history. Why are so many of the London Victorian schools so grandiose in their architecture? Why are some primary schools of the 1930s and 1940s so like country cottages? Why is there so much glass in the schools of the 1970s? The interesting thing about these and many more significant questions is that the time scale of London's mass education system is really remarkably short. Primary education for all from 1870 but secondary education for all only really came in with the 1944 Education Act, while nursery education remains a lottery. with too few places still being a feature of many parts of London. In relation to the teachers in these schools, an all-graduate teaching profession only started to be put in place in the 1960s and its efficacy is still argued over.

A key aspect of this history is the investigation of the demographics of London. Beginning teachers need to have some understanding of where their school students come from. The rapid growth of London was not only the result of internal growth but also of massive immigration. Many London families moved into the city within the last hundred years or so: the concept of 'immigrant' and finding out the push and pull factors behind such movement is a rewarding study, helping to give answers to questions like the one raised earlier, namely as to why these particular school students are in front of this beginning teacher at this time in this school. Such investigations demonstrate that London has always been a multicultural city, as will be seen in this chapter; no educational history of London makes a great deal of sense without that understanding and no contemporary education makes sense without it either.

The history of the inner London boroughs where schools like Hampstead are located needs also to include the range of educational issues stemming from these and other historical changes that have taken place over the last hundred years and their consequent impact upon education. Changes in employment patterns over the last few decades, sometimes both rapid and dramatic, have challenged traditional views of the links between schooling and work and continue to do so. Catchment areas around individual schools can change dramatically in terms of their populations. Perceptions of such areas by those who live there and those who do not, can vary dramatically and change quickly.

Beginning teachers need to be aware of these issues as they greatly influence the learning of their school students.

To make sense of the range of issues, the beginning teachers need access to conceptual tools. History is of course important, but is seldom enough in itself. Beginning teachers need to ask questions about the inner city in which they are working and its impact on the learning of their school students. One such way of looking at the impact of the urban environment upon education could be based on three concepts, namely an understanding of the salient features of

- *Urban function*; i.e. what do cities do? What impact do the industrial, commercial and service industries have on the city and on schooling? What jobs should schools help prepare its young people for? What is the nature of the distinction that is made between education and training, between school and work?

- *Urban form*; i.e. how are they shaped/organised? How do school catchment areas work in the city? Do they continue to have meaning if school students travel half way across London to attend their secondary school? What does the term 'community' mean?

- *Urban meaning*; i.e. what do they mean? There is the city of official statistics and research studies and there is also the city as described by the young people who live in it. Young peoples' perceptions and understandings of the city may well differ from that of their parents and certainly will differ from those of their teachers.

Part of the reasoning behind the beginning teachers' area studies piece of work described earlier in this book was to help bring about this important range of understandings in relation to the context of learning within the school.

These are obviously many other ways of breaking down the complexities of the city. To reiterate a point, however. Much of what the beginning teachers will find out will be in terms of 'what you see depends on where you sit"; in other words, the value system brought to the task will help shape it. Such variation is neither good nor bad but does need the anchor of school actuality, if it is not to remain merely a set of oppositional propositions. School student learning is a useful frame within which to locate and assess the varying perspectives, as personal bias needs to be recognised.

The urban environment is thus a complex one and the beginning teachers can only be introduced to elements of the above discussion. Some of the more detailed work needs to be done in terms of the consequences of these processes that appear to impinge most heavily on inner city teachers (and beginning teachers) and the schools within which they work. Perhaps the most important one relates to the term 'community", a word with a long and sometimes tortured history in London education.

For who can be against community education, long seen as an answer to the perceived anomic and alienating inner city environment? When thinking about initial teacher education and training in cities like London, a more sceptical and less woolly minded stance is required. As a starting point to such a more rigorous stance, there are four main areas to examine with beginning teachers in relation to the term as it is applied to education in such areas, namely, what is meant by the term 'community', how should schools and other urban educational institutions respond to communities, however defined, what is the relationship between the state/wider society, communities, parents and the school and finally, what should all this tell us in relation to initial teacher education and training?

Everybody is in favour of community. Prince Charles and Tony Blair talk and write about restoring and building a sense of community in our society in contradistinction to the self-interest that was espoused in the 1980s. John Major was certainly not against it, whatever this 'it' of community actually is. Sometimes the term seems used as a synonym for what used to be called civic society or even the state. However, in relation to this definitional issue, the important starting point is that its use in education in the inner city is also always seen as benevolent. By calling a failing school a community school, you improve its image if not its effectiveness. (Perhaps the same might be true of those who see Britain as a failing society.) Inner city schools in London like Hampstead may serve many communities, or one, depending on the definition of community that is being used. Unfortunately, there are almost as many definitions of community as there are educationists wishing to use it. Some of the meanings that have been given the word include:

- a group who share a similar, perhaps esoteric interest, such as the intelligence community, hardly a relevant group to inner city education!

- a closed, like-minded group of people, such as are found compulsorily in prisons or voluntarily in monasteries. or compulsorily (school students)and voluntarily (teachers) in schools.

- a group of contiguous people, – a local community, although its boundaries may be rarely agreed upon, either by those inside it, or those outside it. Many people in urban schools refer to their local community in this sense: defined operationally.

- an interest group, eg. against an urban motorway such as the abortive Archway road scheme in North London or parents supporting the ILEA when it was threatened with abolition the first time by Mrs Thatcher's Conservative government. The urban social theorist Manuel Castells defined such groups more accurately as urban social movements (Castells, 1977, 1983).

- a kinship group, either accurately or inaccurately defined. Ian Smith, leader of the illegal government in the last days of Southern Rhodesia

(Zimbabwe) claimed that white Rhodesians, the 'white community'', were 'kith and kin' of the (presumably white) British. Communities thus defined have been the bane of modern European history, but are a feature of racist movements in inner London and consequently have an impact upon education.

- an occupational group, for example mining communities, where the occupation is extended to describe a physical locality. When London still had docks with ships in them, the docking communities existed on both sides of the River Thames.

- the inward looking and potentially xenophobic 'imagined communities' formed as a response to the fractures and uncertainties of modern life, so well analysed by Stuart Hall and his colleagues (Anderson, 1991; Hall *et al.*, 1992). In inner London, much racism springs from such communities, seeing themselves as beleaguered as a result of demographic changes in and near their area, as the fascinating report on racial violence on the Thamesmead Estate in the London Borough of Greenwich reveals (Centre for Multicultural Education, 1992).

One could go on. The literature abounds with definitions, most of which have little in common save a sense of trying to describe structures for human interaction, a pretty broad area. The term also has a long academic history, starting with Tonnies in the 19th century and reaching to Henry Morris and the community college movement of the mid-century in England, particularly in relation to the village colleges of Cambridgeshire.

From this, a broad but vague educational concept has arisen, meaning partly a school's catchment area, and/or the area around the school and/or the various communities that live there or who send children to the school. More importantly, it espouses the whole gamut of home/school/parent/community links and liaisons that have been seen as crucial to successful education in inner city areas. And here, the experience is that successful links in these area does have a beneficial impact on the education that is provided within the school. Parents supporting the reading of their children is perhaps the outstanding example but there are many others. However, it should be noted here that the debate about communities and the debate about parental involvement tend to slide together. Beginning teachers need to know of the crucial importance of parents to the successful education of their children. Most beginning teachers have little difficulty with this: supportive parents are readily seen as having an important part to play in school student learning. Indeed, many of our beginning teachers found attending parents' evenings a valuable and eye opening experience. The wider concept of community links, however, caused them more difficulty, not least because of the conceptual confusion earlier alluded to.

There is also a further set of propositions that have arisen from this confusion about the links between schooling and the community, which the beginning teachers need to be aware of. These are the ways in which the urban community has been conventionally defined by the city educators. One perspective has been to see the community and the school as mutually exclusive and dysfunctional. If the community that supports the school, however defined, is seen as dysfunctional, then the school provides that sense of community that the community cannot provide. The school, within this perspective, becomes a surrogate community, even family. This perspective is based upon a deficit model of education in the inner city and has and retains a powerful hold over many beginning teachers. Images of the undeserving poor and the feckless remain frequent in our imaginations, in contrast to the hard working and deserving poor. The reality is seldom so clear cut, if the initial distinction has indeed, any validity. Without sinking into a relativistic quagmire, it is crucial that beginning teachers are introduced to issues of difference as well as to those of deficit in relation to many of the students that they will be teaching. This is not to say that deficits do not exist: they patently do so, for example in relation to neo-natal nutritional issues, but many seeming deficits are only so because schooling makes them so, as the fierce debates about correct English and English dialects reveal.

Another example would be the view that bilingualism is some form of handicap. One of the exciting things that working with beginning teachers in schools like Hampstead revealed is that attitudes towards bilingualism have significantly shifted, with much more attention being paid to the advantages of bilingualism rather than to the alleged difficulties that bilingualism causes pupils. In addition, seeing bilingualism as an issue of usage rather than competence, loosens up the debate and enables concentration to be placed on issues like the giving of adequate English support to bilingual pupils. Beginning teachers from all subject areas saw this as a crucial aspect of their pedagogic practice and found that the support that the school gave them on this issue was an important benefit of working in this manner in the school. Partly this was because of the reality of the classrooms within which they worked, partly it was a reflection of the many informing discussions they had had with fellow beginning teachers as well as with Institute of Education and school staff.

The alternative to the school as community [dysfunctional community], is seeing the community as a significant educative institution, an idea based on the idea of the dysfunctional school, i.e. a school which discourages rather than encourages learning. Although the beginning teachers saw aspects of school practice that they considered educationally dysfunctional, few of them had much knowledge of alternatives. For example, the 'School in the City' experiments of the 1960s and 1970s in the USA, where school students learned zoology in the city zoo and did drama in the local theatre, proved successful but ultimately failed because they could only be small scale and rarely long term because of other demands on the new types of teachers, who had their full time job to do at the same time. (Perhaps there is a lesson here for those who say that teacher-training can be done solely in schools!) Learning about these experiments fascinated the beginning teachers but seemed to refer not just to a different society but to one where resources were seemingly more plentiful than those they saw around them in the inner city of the 1990s. What they did see, however, was equally interesting, namely the wide range of supplementary schools which surrounded the state schools and which many of the ethnic minority students attended.

Finding out about the range of such community based schools was often a revelation to them. And discussing this range led on to a wide variety of other relevant topics. The supplementary schools with an emphasis on the '3Rs", associated with the African-Caribbean communities, led the beginning teachers to discuss parental expectations as well as the whole range of issues around the achievement levels of African-Caribbeans in the schools. Language and cultural maintenance classes/schools, another form of supplementary education, led to exciting discussions on issues of multilingualism, cultural identity and the role of formal schooling (of which the beginning teachers were now a part) in presenting a particular view of society. Another type of community based education, confessional or religious supplementary schools, such as Quranic and Sunday Schools, raised the issue of religions in school in an open way. In inner London, the school population has a wide range of religious backgrounds. Discussing the range of issues raised was always a fascinating learning experience, though sometime fraught. One of the reasons for this is that active religious belief amongst beginning teachers is a more obvious feature than it was even five years ago. Also, for many schools like Hampstead, the religious beliefs of their students are a much more salient aspect of life than it was comparatively recently. Groups of beginning teachers found that the collaborative working and learning methods adopted on the course made such potentially contentious issues both easy and productive to discuss.

The discussion on the nature of community and the role that education plays was and remains a constant background feature of working with beginning teachers in schools like Hampstead. Questions as to the aims of education are correctly seen as an essential part of initial teacher training/education but have traditionally been too often put over as a set of conflicting abstract principles, seemingly divorced from the reality of classroom survival. An examination of the issues raised by concepts of community make these abstract debates more real and have led to some fascinating discussions as to the purpose of education for individuals and for the community within which they are located. It has also led to the beginning teachers looking at the relevant educational literature in an informed and inquisitive manner. It was refreshing to revisit the extensive post-Plowden community education literature with the benefit of hindsight, particularly the work reporting on Educational Priority Areas (e.g. Halsey, 1972). The beginning teachers quickly found that there were no clear answers in relation to the issues raised by the relationships between schools, school students, their communities and the wider society, leading them to examine even more closely their own aspirations for the students whom they were teaching and also the aspirations for inner London schools that were being expressed by a wide range of other interested parties, from parental and community groups to politicians.

Accepting that this range of views probably could not be readily reconciled is one of the chief difficulties in understanding the urban context within which education takes place. Yet contestation is part of the fabric of education in the inner city and agreements and alliances are constantly shifting. Part of what this means is that inner city schools often have to carry the responsibility for things that are perceived as 'going wrong' in the wider society, a point that will be looked at later in relation to debates about 'going back to basics".

As the preceding discussion on the confusions of community and community education in the inner city indicated, nowhere are contentious areas so pronounced in inner city schools as they are in relation to race and ethnicity. Just as bilingualism has been and will continue to be a constant feature of inner city schools so will the educational issues raised by the fascinating diversity of the pupil population. And debates about such diversity have to be understood within a context of poverty that is such a feature of many inner city areas of London. The booms of the 1970s and 1980s have had little positive impact on many of the inner city areas of London that schools like Hampstead serve. The poverty in these areas and the negative attitudes that this can sometimes engender is a basis for many of the difficulties that schools in such areas face. This is not to argue that teachers do not expect the school students from such disadvantaged backgrounds to succeed in their schools. Far from it. But it does point to the extreme difficulties that some inner city schools face and the need to prepare beginning teachers adequately for work in such schools.

The details of the poverty are alarming. Carey Oppenheim, addressing the inaugural meeting of the London region of the National Local Government Forum in late 1995, revealed that inequality in England was at its most extreme in London. The details that were given were depressing (Cooper, 1995). All but one (the City of London) of the inner London boroughs were on a list of the twenty most deprived boroughs nationally. (The others were Newham, Brent and Waltham Forest, which are outer London Boroughs, the Scilly Isles, Liverpool, Knowsley, Birmingham and Hull.) At ward level, six of the ten most disadvantaged wards were in the inner London borough of Tower Hamlets, the worst ward being Spitalfields, the centre of the Bangladeshi community in Britain, where, amongst other indicators, overcrowding effected nearly 30% of the population as against 1% nationally. More worryingly, Oppenheim reported that the poverty and inequality were increasing. In 1979, household poverty, measured as being half the national average income after housing costs, was 9%. By 1992/3 it was 25%. For children, it was even worse, the rise being from 10% to 33% living in such households: this is 4.3 million children (ibid).

The issues that this raises for ITET in inner London are various and complex. Poverty and school performance still go hand in hand in most cases. Minorities in London are often amongst the poorest inhabitants, as the Spitalfields' figures indicate. However, although this indicates that issues in relation to race and ethnicity are critically important for beginning teachers, the issues involved cannot be disentangled from the educational issues facing white working class children, many of whom are still massive underachievers in inner London schools as the research of Pam Sammons and her colleagues reveals (Sammons, 1994; Sammons et al, 1994). Underachievement is a concern for majority as well as minority students, but the educational disadvantages brought about by xenophobia, discrimination and racism, both overt and covert, are a major concern of many inner city schools and deserve further examination. More than that in the context of this book, it has to be a central concern of any ITET course that hopes to prepare beginning teachers for their work in schools, whether or not they hope to teach in the inner city.

Again, like many other educational issues, beginning teachers need to look back if they are to understand the present. In relation to diversity within city schools, it is essential that beginning teachers have some knowledge of the processes and subsequent history of the movement of people in and around the city. The simple concepts of push and pull factors in relation to migration are easy to understand and are revealing in relation to questions about the student make up in inner city schools. Understanding why groups of people left their home areas (push factors) and why they then came to, say, London (pull factors) is an essential piece of information for teachers who may be faced with some groups of students making chauvinistic and xenophobic comments about who 'belongs' and who does not. Given that just about all Londoners are either immigrants or are descended from immigrants, the issue that has to be put across to students is in relation to the time factors that appear to establish some form of indigenous primacy. As these are clearly arbitrary, the factors that seem to determine indigenous status are more to do with fallacious beliefs about physical appearance and territorial rights, few of which stand up to close scrutiny.

It is therefore really important that beginning teachers have some knowledge of the key elements in this migratory story. In terms of London, this should involve some knowledge of many of the significant minorities, such as the Jews, the Irish, the Travellers and Gypsies, the Welsh, the Scots, the African-Caribbeans, the Indians, the Africans, the Pakistanis, the Cypriots and the Bangladeshis. They should also think about how minorities are categorised and divided – by skin colour, by state of putative origin, by language, by religion and/or by length of residence. And also who does the categorising and dividing: what do terms like Asian or African really mean? Although perhaps unaware of this, the English (whoever they are) appear to follow the line adopted by some states in East and Central Europe, namely by dividing minorities into two broad types: ones that are accepted and ones that are rejected. Interestingly, across Europe, it is the people without a state, like Travellers and Gypsies and until recently, the Jews, who suffer most, followed closely by those who are perceived as being physically different, usually in relation to skin colour.

Schools in inner London like Hampstead have always faced these tensions in a more extreme form than those in most other parts of England and indeed Britain as a whole. They are still part of the intimate texture of every inner London classroom. Partly understood, for complete understanding is all but impossible, these social forces can be harnessed to assist learning, as the beginning teachers saw in many of the lessons that they observed in the school. Ignored, these same social forces can lead to covert and overt racism, damaging the educational development of all concerned.

In addition, understanding of the range of possible educational policy responses to such diversity, as in example from taxonomies such as the assimilation to pluralism one put forward by many writers (e.g. Street-Porter, 1976; Jones, 1992), gives beginning teachers some insights into variation in educational practice within their school and between schools. It is a good example of where greater complexity often brings greater understanding and hopefully, more considered and effective classroom practice.

A key aspect of this effective practice is of course, conventional academic yardsticks, similar to those measured in the Government's academic league tables. Here, the evidence is growing that in London at any rate, some of the minority groups that are most seriously affected by racism are performing well, while others that are less affected, continue to perform badly. Also, it is from the groups that perpetuate racism that some of the worst academic performance is noted (Sammons, op. cit.) The connection between these two variables is at present largely unknown but again, such complexities are valuable, preventing the beginning teachers from making assertions about whole groups of students in relation to the impact of racism on some aspects of learning. What is important in all this, as in so many other educational issues, is that simple singular cause and effect explanations are not really adequate. Amongst other matters, beginning teachers need to collect and assess the evidence in relation to the varying explanations that have been put forward, most of which are usefully discussed in the Swann Report (DES, 1984). The main ones are:

- genetic reasons, mostly developing from the controversial work of Jenson (Jenson, 1969). Central to this area, the debate about the educational differences between black and white school students continues, although few educationalist now support Jensen's thesis (e.g. Blum, 1978; Evans and Waites, 1981; Scarr, 1984)

- unsupportive family structures, a debate that often follows the similar debates about the white working class

- racism, i.e. discrimination, in society and school (Mullard, 1980)

- schools adoption of an unsuitable pedagogic stance. This includes the whole issue of teacher expectations, again a topic that is carefully explored in Green's work, reported in the Swann Report (DES, 1984)

- adverse economic conditions within the family/community, a topic touched on earlier in this chapter.

Discussions with beginning teachers on this topic are always interesting. Furthermore, the issues raised do not apply solely to ethnic minority students but can be discussed in relation to other groups of failing learners, in particular the majority white working class community.

Although the achievement issue is crucial, other issues arise from this school student diversity in inner London, some of them touched upon earlier in the discussion of supplementary schools. Issues relating to language and religious belief are clearly two critical ones here. The number of languages spoken in inner London schools alone is estimated at over two hundred, making London perhaps the most linguistically diverse city in the world (ILEA, 1989). In relation to religion, apart from the long standing debate about whether school should practice religious education or religious instruction, beginning teachers need to also engage with the separate schools debate as well as having some knowledge of the main elements of the religions represented in their own school. As was mentioned earlier on in the book, when looking at the Area Study undertaken by the beginning teachers, finding this information was fascinating in itself as well as being useful in relation to actual classroom practice.

Finally, the discussion of racism in education can often be located in broader discussions of bullying and other anti-social behaviour within schools. The extent of bullying in all schools tends to be understated and under-reported but it is of great importance to understanding barriers to learning generally in schools. As could be anticipated, its discussion has led to some of the most demanding sessions with the beginning teachers. This was because, like most teachers, they were aware of it but felt that they seldom saw or recognised it, for much bullying consists of a constant stream of seemingly trivial acts that teachers frequently overlook or misinterpret.

Like many other issues that came their way, this, and the other complexities of the inner city and its impact upon school life are a never ceasing debate between the beginning teachers and their mentors and tutors. The debates about community, diversity, poverty and the relationship between these broader concepts and the practice of teaching mean that the beginning teachers are constantly assessing their own practice, as well as the practice of others. This particular aspect of their learning also challenged many of the assumptions that they bring to it, irrespective of their own political biases.

So far, this chapter has been arguing for the need to confront beginning teachers with the complexity of the inner city and the impact of this complexity upon education. However, this very complexity poses other key dilemmas. This chapter is not putting forward a postmodern relativistic agenda for dealing with these complexities. It is arguing that the late modern agenda of rationality and deliberation in regard to education is not discredited but should be seen as more complex than it is sometimes assumed to be. As Giroux puts it:

> Modernism is far from dead – its central categories are simply being written within a plurality of narratives that are attempting to address the new set of social, political, technical and scientific configurations that constitute the current age. (Giroux, 1991, p. 63)

A similar point is made by Bauman, albeit writing from a postmodern perspective:

> Postmodernity may be conceived of as a modernity conscious of its true nature – *modernity for itself.* The most conspicuous features of the post-modern condition: institutionalised pluralism, variety, contingency and ambivalence – have all been turned out by modern society in ever increasing volumes; yet they were seen as signs of failure rather than success... (Bauman,1993, pp. 187-188)

Following this argument, plurality and complexity are the prevailing features of urban societies and their schools but are too frequently seen as problems rather than opportunities. And it is by seeing the complexity in this latter way that beginning teachers can begin to appreciate not just the vibrant excitement of working in inner city schools but also the potential for providing valid and successful education for their students.

A key educational aspect of such a new view of the inner city school is the concept of a plurality of explanations or narratives and an understanding of the power of dominant ones. The issues such a viewpoint opens up go to the heart of the English education system. The many nationalities and/or groups con-tained within the schools of cities like London are still too often ignored or submerged beneath an increasingly anglocentric curriculum. As Bhabha claims:

> It is the mark of the ambivalence of the nation as a narrative strategy – and an apparatus of power – that it produces a continual slippage into analogous, even metonymic, categories, like the people, minorities or 'cultural difference' that continually overlap in the act of writing the nation. (Bhabha, 1990, p. 293)

Such myths and narratives of urban, national, state, community and European identity are, in fact, partly a codification and legitimation of the dominant group[s] social and economic arrangements and partly a reflection of dominant concepts of the nature of all of these groupings. In other words, the ambiguities and dilemmas that beginning teachers are beginning to face during their training do not point to a new social agenda, but argue for greater clarification and under-standing of the existing agenda, – of a sophisticated rationality that attempts to provide a good education in inner city schools despite the complexities that are beginning to be discovered.

The issues that arise for urban schools and ITET in relation to this confusion are complex and difficult to handle. One way forward is to accept and teach about, not just the contingent, plural nature of London's schools and indeed English/British society but also the concept of individual plural identities for individuals at the local, national and international level. Stuart Hall sums it all up succinctly when he states:

> The fully unified, completed, secure and coherent identity is a fantasy. Instead, as the systems of meaning and cultural representation multiply, we are confronted by a bewildering, fleeting multiplicity of possible identities, any one of which we could identify with... (Hall, 1992, p. 277)

Such complexity is frightening at one level. Faced with it, many people with an interest in education (and social life generally) retreat from its consequences. The consensus of the post-war period in education broke down as a con-sequence. The failure of planning, in education as elsewhere, meant for some that all planning was wrong, with the market being the only fair form of social and educational adjudication. Its primary British exponent was Sir Keith Joseph, Margaret Thatcher's guru and one time Minister of Education in one of her administrations. He asserted

> The blind, unplanned, uncoordinated wisdom of the market....is over-whelmingly superior to the well researched, rational, systematic, well mean-ing, co-operative, science based, forward looking, statistically respectable plans of governments... (Quoted in Jones, 1989, p.46)

Applying this 'blind, unplanned, uncoordinated wisdom of the market' was one major plank in the 1988 Education Act, although it is interesting to note that that same government was initially reluctant to relinquish control of ITET to similar forces and indeed has never relinquished control of the curriculum. Such pure free market philosophy was difficult to sustain, particularly for politicians whose major *raison d'etre* is intervention. Many inner city schools cannot thrive in a free market and concerns about young peoples' behaviour cannot easily be laid at the door of their schools.

So, if many inner city schools are said to be failing and the complexities of modern life are claimed to increasing, how best should education be regarded? Sir Keith Joseph's despair over rationality and his optimism over the market has clearly been one influential response, although its almost Messianic clarity has been avoided by most politicians who actually have power. Three other strands of response can, however, be identified in the debate over inner city schools. Two are similar to Joseph's, in that they signal retreat from the complexity. The first of these two is religious fundamentalism, returning to the eternal verities. This should not be read as an attack on religion, more a warning about some more extreme manifestations of religious belief and practice that seek to impose themselves on educational practice. However, such a returning to religious roots can cause real dilemmas for inner city schools, as current debates about the place of Islam and Christianity in many such schools indicates. Such practice also reveal dilemmas in relation to the rights of parents to inculcate funda-mentalist beliefs in their children and the rights of the child to develop its own autonomy. Both rights are enshrined in UN Declarations but at heart, they are incompatible.

Similar to the retreat into religious fundamentalism is an even woollier version of this form of escape. In its almost endearingly English form, it is the 'back to basics' movement put forward by John Major, the British Prime Minister in the early 1990s. As Coulby and Jones put it, this approach

> Characterised by the slogan 'Back to Basics', it faced the dilemmas of the late modern social and educational agenda by commanding them to go away with a Canute-like gesture. In speeches and interviews, he evoked a vision of England and English life as a revival of as a 1930s suburban lifestyle of bliss and order. That this was a myth and potentially a dangerous one had been exposed by Lewis Mumford who argued that the 'suburb served as an asylum for the preservation of illusion. Here domesticity could flourish, forgetful of the exploitation on which so much of it was based. Here individuality could prosper, oblivious of the pervasive regimentation beyond. This was not merely a child-centred environment, it was based on a childish view of the world...' (Mumford, 1961, p. 563.) If back to basics is indeed, 'a childish view of the world', it retains significant educational power. Its educational touchstones in the UK include spelling tests, an attack on real books as an aid to reading, formal teaching methods, school uniform, streaming, selection and, if European law would only allow it, corporal punishment. These beliefs and practices were also the basis of the UK's mass education system in the nineteenth and first half of the twentieth century. (Coulby and Jones, 1995, p. 144)

The third strand, which might be termed a toolmaker response, looks set to be a return to the consensus of the 1960s and 1970s, albeit in a much modified form. It is about school improvement and school effectiveness. From this perspective, urban schools are frequently inefficient and ineffective but the criteria for effectiveness and efficiency are known and just need implementation. A fairy story may make this clearer.

A left wing, interventionist government is elected in Britain and decides to tackle the issues of poor quality schooling in the inner city. It argues, against much research evidence to the contrary (e.g. Bourdieu and Passeron, 1977; Halsey et al., 1980), that there is no reason why the children in such schools should not do as well as those attending leafy suburban schools provided the education that is offered to them is efficient and effective. It starts its reforms by acknowledging the hard work and dedication of many of those who teach in such schools. It also acknowledges that resource starvation, low pay and low morale has meant that there are some inadequate teachers in the same schools, such teachers giving a really poor deal to their school students. Poor quality teaching and school leadership are seen as key elements to be tackled if these inadequacies are to be effectively dealt with. The same government initiative would argue that urban working class and ethnic minority parents are denied information about what is happening in their schools, preventing such parents from making well informed choices about schools and subjects and that this information denial must be remedied. Their freedom of choice should be enhanced to the levels already enjoyed by many middle class parents. To help in this, there is a public national curriculum, while value added league tables of schools would be published annually. In addition, frequent outside and impartial inspection of schools and the publication of their findings should be introduced to help bring about the needed changes. During the inspections, good teachers and good headteachers should be identified and recognition given to them: poor teachers and poor headteachers should also be identified and plans drawn up to help them improve the quality of their work. If the quality does not improve, they will need to be replaced, for the sake of the children they are currently failing. In addition, the factors identified in ILEA sponsored research into effective schooling (e.g. Rutter *et al.*, 1979; Hargreaves *et al.*, 1984: Mortimore *et al.*, 1988), would be the basis for further research and detailed implementation in schools. Finally, ITET would be based on a genuine and properly funded partnership between schools and HEIs. It is a tough programme and will face considerable opposition from powerful vested interests, probably right wing, in education. In broad outline, however, it is what the last Conservative government attempted to do. In other words, a new educational consensus seems to have arrived. Whether it will be any more successful than the consensual educational policies of the 1960s and 1970s is a moot point.

The fairy story indicates a somewhat sceptical approach to this new consensus. However, it surely has to be approved, as it is better than what has gone immediately before. More positively, the improvements brought about by the exponents of school improvement are clearly worthwhile and need to be supported. But debates about school knowledge, about the impact of social class, race, religion, disability and language on educational achievement in the broadest sense of that word need to be maintained and supported too. Furthermore, it is crucial that beginning teachers are introduced to these issues also, if we are to have an active, responsive and flexible teaching force in the next century.

Inner city education has always posed difficulties for the system and the society in which it is located. Radical thinking is constantly needed. The preparation of teachers for work in such areas has to be exemplary and has to involve a real partnership between school and HEI, a point discussed further in Appendix 3. It has to be well thought out, efficient and adventurous, challenging and at bottom, deeply rooted in a concern for successful practice.

CHAPTER 14

THE QUALITY OF OUR LEARNING: WAYS FORWARD

Crispin Jones

As urban society gains in complexity and confusion, teachers are increasingly in the forefront of public attention. While teachers actually attempt to prepare young people for an uncertain future, 'back seat teacher' politicians of all hues are all too ready to blame them for failing to prepare young people adequately for the world that they will have to live in and take responsibility for. One consequence of this continual blaming of teachers, especially those in urban areas, is that recruitment to teaching is falling just as the need for greater numbers of teachers is becoming more apparent. Thus, one of the important things about learning how to teach in inner city schools like Hampstead is that because the excitement of teaching and learning permeates the school, it helps counteract much of this negative and unhelpful criticism. Yet, preparing teachers for their complex task gets more difficult by the day and is not helped by simplistic explanations and solutions put forward by people in authority in education and elsewhere.

The increasing demands on teachers come from a range of sources and it is worth noting some of the more important ones. At a simple technical level, the changes brought about by the introduction of the National Curriculum and the range of other changes brought about by the 1988 Education Act and its successor education acts and ministerial fiats have placed enormous new demands on teachers, which they are only just coming to terms with and taking control of. Teachers in Hampstead, as in every other school in England, have had to deal with, absorb and effectively teach a curriculum which has changed with bewildering rapidity over the last eight or so years. That they have been so effective and can communicate their effectiveness to new teachers partly gives the lie to much of the negative comment that has been made about teachers' competences and commitment mentioned earlier.

To such curricula vision and revision has to be coupled the rapid and increasing changes in the actual knowledge that lies at the base of the curriculum, which teachers have to try and keep abreast of. Major advances in the sciences are well known but there have been important new perspectives in all curriculum subjects over the last twenty or so years. Subjects like History and Geography have changed as much as Physics and Chemistry as subjects of study at university. Inevitably, however, there is a lag between such new knowledge and its entrance into the school curriculum. Such a lag has the virtue of ensuring that passing academic fashion is kept out of the curriculum as far as is possible but has the weakness of allowing inappropriate and even fallacious knowledge to continue to be taught. In addition, whole new areas of knowledge have appeared in the school, most noticeably IT. Although nearly all beginning teachers come to their education courses with some IT skills, nearly all require more, given the pace of change in that field. Thirty years' ago, secondary schools were full of classes of [mainly] girls, learning how use typewriters; there might have been a computer terminal in the Maths or Science department, a few Gestetner and Banda copying machines and a few phones. The personal computer revolution, photocopiers and fax machines were yet to come. Now, nobody can really guess what the IT changes in the next decade are likely to be, save for the fact that they will be massive and expensive. Preparing beginning teachers for this future is not easy but has to be a major concern for teacher education, a point that is well demonstrated in Chapter 5.

Beginning teachers frequently have other knowledge deficits to make up during their training. Degree courses have become more specialised, particularly in the Sciences, and beginning teachers have to find the time during their crowded time to learn or re-learn significant areas of the curriculum that they will have to teach. Here they rely very heavily on the good will and expertise of their departmental colleagues, which although freely given, is another demand being made upon already busy teachers.

Similar rapid changes are taking place in relation to pedagogy. If one of the purposes of teacher education is to make a beginning teacher aware of pedagogies other than those which are familiar from their own schooling, then schools like Hampstead, with its pragmatic but intellectually grounded pedagogic debates, are a crucial supporter of the work that is done in the higher education institution (HEI) by the beginning teacher's tutors who are working there. But pedagogic change is not simply an academic issue. Apart from traditionalist views of what an appropriate pedagogy is, most in education see that an appropriate pedagogy, especially in inner city schools, needs to consist of a wide, effective repertoire of skills and techniques based on both a knowledge of how young people learn and the range of factors that can impact upon that learning.

Principal amongst these framing factors is the rapid pace of societal change and the increasing dislocation of social life, particularly in our inner cities – a point taken up particularly in the previous chapter. Some of these changes have a major impact upon learning and thus pose new questions for beginning teachers to tease out. Whether we are in a late modern or a postmodern stage of development is an important debate but is less important for the beginning teacher than is recognising the features of contemporary social change that will impinge upon their work (Coulby and Jones, 1995). For example, traditional forms of authority are increasingly questioned, including those in schools. Keeping discipline has never been easy in inner city schools, as the work of Gerald Grace interestingly demonstrates (Grace, 1979). It is certainly a perennial issue for established teacher and beginning teacher alike. In an era struggling with relativism, the issues for teachers are increasingly difficult. The official government position, perhaps best expressed by Dr Nicholas Tate, head of the School Curriculum and Assessment Authority, is to reject late modernity and return to the old, so-called certainties. He argues for four guiding principles in this complex area of education (Tate, 1996).

- A basic purpose of education is to help students to appreciate and sustain 'the best of our cultural inheritance' (ibid. p.18)

- '...the curriculum needs to be firmly and proudly rooted in a cultural heritage with its roots in Greece and Rome, in Christianity and in European civilisation.... Hence the centrality of British history, Britain's changing relations with the rest of the world, the English literary heritage (with Shakespeare in pride of place) and the study of Christianity, alongside the development of critical skills' (ibid.)

- 'Third, that all pupils should be made aware of the rich heritage of some of the other cultural traditions now [emphasis added] represented in this country.' (ibid.)

- 'The final big idea is that we should aim to develop in young people a sense that some works of art, music, literature or architecture are more valuable than others... By the post-modern view there are no differences in value between, say, Schubert's Ave Maria and the latest Blur release, or between Milton and Mills and Boon. The final big idea therefore, is that a key purpose of the curriculum is to introduce young people to some of the characteristics of what traditionally has been known as 'high culture', the pursuit of knowledge for its own sake. I am not saying that young people should spend all their time studying Jane Austen and Shakespeare or listening to Bach and Mozart. What I am suggesting is that we, their educators, should give these things their proper value, as, in Mathew Arnold's words 'the best that has been known and thought' (Tate, quoted in Charter, 1996. p.7).

Tate is worth quoting at length because, by virtue of his office, he is currently so influential in terms of what beginning teachers are supposed to have as a framework within which a curriculum is delivered. He is surely correct that all teachers have to have a clear moral, aesthetic and spiritual stance: he is, equally, surely incorrect to assert a notion of an accepted English culture that is clearly defined and to claim a moral primacy for an undefined and probably undefinable concept of European civilisation (Coulby and Jones, op.cit.).

Tate is also helpful because he makes it clear that the demands on young teachers are likely to increase in these areas. To any individual beginning teachers' personal stance on these crucial issues has to be added the stress that is raised for them in a contemporary classroom by its complex diversity in terms of the issues that Tate raises. Beginning teachers have to clarify for themselves and their charges a range of such crucial issues, while at the same time worrying about accusations of indoctrination. It is an issue made the more difficult with indoctrination frequently being seen as the teaching of opinions others disagree with.

When working with beginning teachers, these issues often have to take second place to seeming more pressing questions. However, increasingly they have to be a key part of their work in schools like Hampstead. But as always in initial education and training, the issue boils down to the twin questions of funding and time. The one year PGCE is a gallop with many interested parties wanting their share of the time. In the 1980s, there was an attempt to save time and improve quality by a systematic attack on the value of theory in initial training and education. Thankfully, this mistaken view has mainly been discredited. Now, debates about competences and their assessment, although important and valuable, need to include a wider range of expectations than has previously been the case in government thinking about teacher education.

A strong example of this in urban schools is in the area of pastoral care, in particular the Personal and Social Education/ Personal, Social and Health Education curriculum (PSHE/PSE). A teacher's formal concern with the range of issues which have been reviewed, namely the complicated educational issues associated with moral, spiritual and aesthetic development are mainly dealt with through a school's pastoral system. Increasingly, NQTs are becoming pastoral tutors in the first year of teaching but are still seldom prepared for this crucial role. At Hampstead, this concern has been considered but not to the extent which seems necessary. However, if more time is given to it, what gets left out?

The developing partnerships in initial teacher education and training may contain some of the answers to this and other questions. As this has developed over the last few years, new and exciting possibilities emerge each year, as Leon Gore's chapter revealed. HEIs have become more open to schools with benefit (and costs) to both. (Some views on this are given in Appendix 3.) The increasing involvement of central government is welcomed in theory, as it indicates the commitment of the state to providing high quality education and training for our teachers. In conjunction with good LEA support, the stage is set for a fruitful four-way partnership in the near future.

Such a partnership has a further axis, namely the increasing perception of the formalising and structuring of a teacher's professional development from beginning teacher, to NQT, to experienced teacher – right through to preparation for headship and development of that role from within it. As Tamsyn Imison, the Head of the school, indicated in this book, a school only makes sense if everyone there sees themselves as learners as well as teachers. The new career entry profiles perhaps mark the beginning of this greater formalisation and commitment to professional development.

One final point needs making: it is not the intention of the model of initial teacher education that this book describes to produce clones of those providing it. There is no clear model of the ideal teacher, as a moment's reflection on one's own education would confirm. This book is an attempt to show what happens in one inner city school. We believe that it works in this context but it is not a definitive map of the field.

EXTRACTS FROM THE HEADTEACHER'S STATEMENT TO OFSTED

Tamsyn Imison

Intake

We have traditionally taken school students from over 50 feeder primary schools but this number has now dropped to 40 as the school has become more popular and the catchment area has reduced to under one mile radius. (We have over 120 children on the waiting list for next September.) 27% of our intake are entitled to free school meals and 36% have single parent status. There are 40 statemented school students , 3% of our roll. 176 other students are on the SEN register at stages 2-4 comprising 13% of our roll.

School students' prior attainment

Over the years the broad spread and balance of attainment levels have been maintained and we take a true comprehensive mix with 25% of Band 1, 50% from Band 2 and 25% from Band 3. However there is a difference between the levels for boys and girls with more girls in band 1 and more boys in band 3. The ILEA banding by verbal reasoning and London Reading Test finished in 1989 but we have used the London Reading Test since 1990 as a guide to the intake levels of school students. This is being extended in 96/97 to include verbal reasoning and mathematical tests to augment the inadequate information from Key Stage 2 SATS results. 20% of our present year 7 intake have a reading score two or more years below their chronological age.

Relevant Staffing Issues

Staffing has always been my top priority – appointing, developing and supporting excellent personnel. Over the years the quality of staff appointed has been high but there was a serious problem during the period of the ILEA Redeployment exercise when staff were drafted into schools without Governors or Headteacher involvement. This has meant that we have had to give considerable time and effort to pressure and support, leading in some cases to extended disciplinary proceedings. The previous Head of Religious Education was placed in the school in 1987 by the ILEA and, following all appropriate procedures eventually left the school on December 31st 1995. During this time great efforts were made to put a Religious Education Programme together but the materials and schemes of work were not acceptable to the school or to the Inspectorate. We are at long last in the situation where we can rethink the place of Religious Education and redesign the school shadow structure so that a new appointment can be made which ensures that the school complies with statutory requirements and meets the needs of all students. This will go along with the restructuring and development of the whole pastoral and academic support system which is one of our key School Development Plan targets. A new appointment within my Deputies is also imminent as a result of a Senior Executive Restructure which was designed to facilitate support in this area .

Monitoring achievement

I have been monitoring examination results since I arrived in 1984 and they have shown a pleasing steady rise. Camden used NFER to analyse the 1995 results in Camden schools for value added and this indicated a significant value added component in all three core subjects in our school. Boys' results were a cause for concern in comparison to our girls' results but targeting has lifted them in 1995 to a level on a par with those of girls.

Site constraints

The school is on a very cramped site. The three buildings fronting the road were built in 1897 for Haberdasher Aske's Boys. The 'New' block at the rear was built for the opening in 1961 of a new comprehensive. The practical problems we face are due to: 1. spaces appropriate to classes of 15 in a small independent boys' school 2. the 60's building having an expected functional span of only 35 years 3. Teaching spaces which are either very cramped or too large.

We have managed to get Camden LEA to split one large laboratory into two good newly fitted labs and work is starting on a similar conversion on the top floor which will provide a much needed additional practical space. Currently a significant number of Science lessons have to be taught in non- specialist rooms. We also have times during the week when every teaching space is taken. We have to bus school students to playing fields in Mill Hill for PE although recently I have been able to hire the small all-weather pitch at the top of the University College School playing fields adjacent to our site.

There are no other secondary schools within our catchment area and the FE College is in the opposite corner of the Borough, which means there is pressure for our sixth form places as we have no viable consortia options. The school would like to increase the sixth form roll from 230 to 300 if the site could be creatively developed. Camden LEA is paying for a feasibility study to look at this and tendering is underway.

Some of our achievements

- very high staying on rates post 16 as a result of a long-standing active policy of encouraging school students to go on with their education

- a climate of learning across the school where teachers want to learn and develop

- equal opportunities demonstrated by strong role models and targeted support eg boys' achievement rising by 10% last year in GCSE

- evaluation of our last School Development Plan showed that we had achieved all the targets set on Attendance and Punctuality, on Differentiation and on Assessment

- improved examination results again with 52% of our school students gaining 5 or more A-C (46% in 94) above Camden average of 37.3% and national (43.5%) This was achieved even with a large compulsory core for all school students ahead of National Curriculum requirements

- boys' results at GCSE improving considerably to 52% (33.7% in 1993; 39.3 % in 1994) on a par with girls' results

- major Community library plans where the school has already raised £55,000 and earmarked saving to match this

- working with several International Property Advisers on a major PFI initiative for site developments for the next millennium

Our school statement of intent has arisen from successive statements as a result of whole staff, school student, parent and Governor consultation.

The Statement of Intent states:

At Hampstead School everyone will strive to:

- enjoy the challenges and achievements of learning

- develop individual strengths

- experience academic, social and personal success

- manage setbacks

- develop consideration and co-operation

within a stimulating and supportive environment and with the support of family and the wider community.

Task Groups

There are task groups for each whole school objective. Each task group has a clear brief, related to the development plan, and reports back to whole staff meetings each term. An important function of the task groups is to make specific proposals for the following year's action plans. The Parent Governors are supported by the Governing Body and the Senior Executive in establishing a task group to enlist the more active involvement of parents in the work of the school and to ensure that communications are parent friendly and meet parents' expressed needs for information.

Lesson Observation

All staff and governors are involved in a rolling programme of lesson observation. Lesson observation is a valuable tool for measuring the qualitative aspects of school development and for ensuring that the SDP is making a difference to teaching and learning. It encourages professional dialogue and fosters a shared understanding of the school's values and practices. The findings of lesson observation will be co-ordinated by the Lesson Observation Task Group and the outcomes fed back to Senior Executive, governors and staff.

Evaluation

At the beginning of the next academic year, Heads of Departments / Heads of Year and Task Group leaders will produce an evaluation of progress within their areas. The Senior Executive will also evaluate the whole school action plans and check whether or not we have met our targets for the year.

Whole School Objectives for 1995-98

Objective A: to ensure that all school students have access to a challenging and appropriate curriculum

Key Actions:

- further develop differentiation across the curriculum and ensure that it is evident in schemes of work and syllabuses which will be given high visibility with school students and parents

- audit cross-curricular development of IT, literacy and Numeracy skills and develop a more co-ordinated and systematic programme in all curriculum areas

- review current programme of Personal, Social and Health Education provision and implement a new structure, to include assemblies and school student conferences

- implement the Special Educational Needs Code of Practice

- enhance the learning environment by improving classroom, display and departmental facilities.

Objective B: to ensure that we have an assessment system which benefits school students, parents and teachers

Key Actions:
- establish a schedule of work reviews for each year group and improve the systems for school student assessment, self-assessment and target-setting

- produce departmental portfolios to illustrate standards at each Key Stage

- introduce the Year 11 Information Service (YELIS) and the A Level Information Service (ALIS)

- introduce a new commendation system including more public recognition and reward for achievement

- improve the system for reporting to parents

Objective C: to develop the school as a learning community

Key Actions:
- involve all teaching and support staff in 'Investors in People'

- establish a lesson observation programme in order to share good practice

- schedule a programme of events to involve parents more fully in the work of the school

- extend extra-curricular activities and monitor effect on achievement

- develop a community library, including an Independent Learning Centre

Targets

In setting our school targets we have taken account of the National Targets for Education and Training for the Year 2000, 'Developing skills for a successful future'. Our targets spell out our expectations and will enable us to measure the effect of our developments on school student achievement.

Foundation Learning
- By age 19, 85% of young people to achieve 5 GCSEs at Grade C or above, an Intermediate GNVQ or an NVQ level 2.

- 75% of young people to achieve level 2 competence in communication and numeracy and 35% to achieve level 3 competence in these core skills by age 21. And IT by age 19;

- By age 21, 60% of young people to achieve 2 GCE A Levels, an Advanced GNVQ or an NVQ level 3.

Lifetime Learning

- 70% of all organisations employing 200 or more employees, and 35% of those employing 50 or more, to be recognised as Investors in People.

- Individual departments have also set targets that are specific to both their subject and particular groups of school students.

The school has recently taken the decision to subscribe to ALIS (A Level Information Service) and YELIS (Year 11 Information Service). In future years, this will supply us with more accurate, contextual data against which to set our targets. However, we felt it was important that we should make a start on target-setting rather than wait for this information. Targets may be adjusted as this information becomes available.

CODE OF PRACTICE FOR THE PLACEMENT OF BEGINNING TEACHERS AT HAMPSTEAD SCHOOL

Ruth Heilbronn

- As a rule **no class may have more than two trainee teachers** over the year, and across all curriculum subjects. There may be the odd exception. All timetables to be issued to the School Training Co-ordinator for monitoring and co-ordination

- **Trainee teachers to be fully supported** in the classroom and with every aspect of the training and induction over the year. Namely, the teacher timetabled to be in charge of the class taken by the trainee teacher to be available within calling distance at all times. **Timetabled teachers are legally responsible for their classes, both pedagogically and for health and safety.**

The initial induction period for trainee teachers may last until the last two weeks of the first teaching practice. Timetabled teachers must work out lessons to proceed in the following **stages**:

- **The trainee teacher sits in with the class and observes.** S/he may work with small groups of school students.

- The trainee teacher continues to observe and work with small groups and **addresses the whole class for the part of the lesson**. Lesson planning with the timetabled teacher to have included negotiation, induction, training as preparation for this.

- The trainee teacher **team teaches** with the timetabled teacher – the timetabled teacher having worked out the lesson jointly with the trainee.

- In the last weeks of the first practice the trainee teacher should **take responsibility for the whole class** – the timetabled teacher should **remain with the class** initially or within earshot. The timetabled teacher's observations and advice based on observations are important parts of the training process. The class also deserve and need their timetabled teacher's attention. The timetabled teacher is irreplaceable at this point. The trainee teacher is an additional resource, who is being trained alongside the timetabled teacher.

A log needs to be kept by the timetabled teachers of their work with the trainees – a proforma will be issued. This is necessary for the assessments. Logs to be filed in trainee teachers' files. The log will be extremely brief notes eg

> 20/9/94   'Discussed composition of group, gave register, set observation time'.

A file on each trainee teacher needs to be kept in the department with open records available when required. Teachers' logs of their meetings with trainee teachers to be kept in here. Subject supervisors will monitor the file and keep their own co-ordinated log.

Trainee teachers should be given **keys, photocopy cards, access to facilities they need to prepare lessons** – (Budget holder – RH, Training budget)

They have the **right to quality time.**

Trainee teachers have to assist the timetabled teacher and the department in any reasonable way – e.g. preparing materials, assisting with clubs, visits NB. They have access to their university libraries and resource and media resource centres, video loans etc. and can be asked to bring resources into school. The partnership with the Higher Education Institutions is two way.

THE POTENTIAL ROLE OF HEIs
Crispin Jones

The focus of this book has been on Hampstead School as a training institution for beginning teachers. However, this education and training is a partnership with HEIs. These too, need to reassess their role in relation to education and training for teachers in urban schools. Given that, what ought an HEI be looking to be as it faces the challenges of the next century, when cities and their schools are likely to become even more complex structures? Such a model would have a range of criteria that it ought to meet. The main ones might be the following:

- knowledge and understanding of current educational policy developments, particularly in relation to the education and training of teachers for work in urban schools

- clarity of understanding of the central areas of work of an institution that trains such teachers

- awareness of possible future developments in cities and their likely implications for education

- understanding of current thinking and practice with regard to effective educational management and leadership, i.e. the new consensus discussed elsewhere in this book.

Given those, what are likely to be the salient features of a successful HEI training institution in the next century and what strategies will have been adopted to have brought this about? One way of looking at these issues is to set benchmarks of success. If that is done, there is a need to delineate it in terms of success along two axes, namely the *quality* of the work undertaken and the *key activities*, by level and type.

In terms of *quality*, a successful HEI training institution will be

- professionally respected and approved

- innovative and

- economically viable.

In terms of key *activities*, a successful HEI training institution will be involved, in partnership with schools and LEAs, in, *inter alia*:

- the education and initial training of teachers

- the further professional development of teachers, including headteacher development

- educational research and its dissemination.

These outlines need amplification. In terms of quality, a successful HEI will be one that responds to change without sacrificing or abandoning quality. It will be, as a consequence, professionally respected and approved. Such professional respect is essential, for without it there would be no HEI training. Student numbers are the lifeblood of a successful HEI system and are increasingly the result of a range of professional approval ratings, such as teaching quality, course excellence and a relevant and/or innovative research profile. An institution with a reputation for providing quality teachers to London's schools will not lack good quality applicants for its courses and good placements for its beginning teachers and NQTs. In addition, initial training is increasingly controlled by professional opinion outside of the HEI training institutions themselves and this is most unlikely to change over the next five or so years. It is indeed, a part of a more general concern for a quality audit across the whole higher education sector and needs to be seen as enhancing quality rather than detracting from it.

The second element denoting quality would be the institution's innovative stance. A successfully innovative education and training HE institution might be characterised by the following features

- organisational structures that are proactive rather than reactive

- an institutional ethos that has accepted and built on the necessary tension between administrative and academic priorities

- a staff development model that focuses on individual growth as well as on institutional need. There is also likely to be a promotion policy in place, that recognises and rewards teaching and administration as well as research

- a staff resource/accountability model that is perceived as transparent and equitable

- quality control mechanisms that are seen as responsive and effective in terms of the quality that they define and ensure, as well as the time that is spent upon them

- a learning resources/IT strategy.

The third element representing quality seems on the face of it, an odd choice, namely, that the institution has to be economically viable. Few training institutions can ignore the market. There is no doubt that economically non-viable activities, whatever their abstract worth, cannot be supported over the medium term by successful HE training institutions. New initiatives have to be encouraged but this will frequently mean some cut backs in other areas of work which are seen as being no longer viable. It also means that imaginative and professionally valid responses have to react to demands made from influential outside agencies, particularly governmental ones.

In areas where the HEI has some control over fee levels, and this is likely to increase as the idea of the market is espoused by [or forced upon] it, a successful institution will have a clear strategy in relation to its potential markets, collaborators and competitors. Part of this will support revenue-earning initiatives, such as specialised short courses, that will help other activities, particularly those in their development phases. A successful HEI in teacher education is also likely to be one that marks out areas for student and research growth, so-called academic niches. Improving the quality of training for work in inner city schools is one such area.

Three key activities were also found. The most important is, of course the education and initial training of teachers. Training teachers is one of the main purposes of a successful training institution and hopefully will remain so. A research led educational HEI education and training institution is unlikely to be successful as examples from the USA demonstrate. However, the place of such training within the HE system will continue to need defending. This is despite the fact that education, broadly defined, has always been a central concern of HE. The abolition of Faculties, Schools, Departments and Institutes of Education would not mean the end of this study, just as they were never a prerequisite for it. Furthermore, if universities and certain other HE institutions have traditionally been seen as elite institutions, part of their work has always been the preparation (and in some cases, training) of students for elite occupations such as the priesthood, medicine and law. Old (e.g. architects and teachers) and new (e.g. computer programmers and social workers) occupational groups seeking to enhance their status and remuneration have successfully persuaded successive governments to fund their training in such elite institutions because such training would improve the quality of service offered. In the main, the older universities have resisted these demands while the newer ones have embraced them.

Despite this resistance, the belief is now widespread that degree level qualifications are an essential part of the training for a wide range of occupational groups. While the desirability of extended higher educational opportunities for all seems relatively non-problematic, the extension of university-based occupational training is seen as much more contentious. Generally speaking, 'my' occupation deserves such training, as do those occupations seen as being equal or superior to 'mine'. Occupations perceived as inferior are clear signs of the dilution of standards. Postgraduate training of morticians and beauty therapists (hairdressers) exist in the USA but are seen as lowering the tone, except by morticians and beauty therapists.

If the purposes and practices of education have long been studied, albeit not exclusively in universities, the link between these studies and the training of teachers in the same or similar institutions is less clear. Obviously the insights gleaned from the first activity should influence the second but it is more questionable whether the same people or the same institution should be involved in the two processes. In education, we are increasingly fudging the issue by calling our teacher training 'teacher education' and resisting the notion of training, perhaps to the detriment of the needs of beginning teachers and the schools they will be working in.

The increasing complexity of the division of labour in the study of education also appears to suggest that it is increasingly difficult for individuals to pursue efficiently all three activities (research, teaching and occupational training), despite their inter-relationship. The system currently rewards each activity differentially: it has always done so and while such activities take place within the single institution it will probably continue to do so. Institutional separation, however, will do nothing to change this and will fossilise existing status differentials. Within a single institution, career development has the potential to ensure that people work at the activities that are most rewarding for them and for their institution, as well as accepting that these might well change over an individual's career. It has to be admitted that institutional and personal preferences can only be matched with great difficulty and that institutional flexibility appears to be decreasing due to financial imperatives.

The second key activity that was identified was the further professional development of teachers. A shortage of well qualified teachers to work in inner city areas is likely to remain a feature of the educational landscape in the next century. Among other things, this means that INSET provision is crucial to the improvement of the educational service in such areas. The success of the GEST 16 courses run by LEAs in relation to supporting bilingual students in mainstream classrooms is an excellent contemporary example. The newly evolving partnerships between school, colleges, LEAs and training institution will have an impact on all such aspects of the professional development of teachers. A successful training institution, particularly one that hope to serve the urban schooling system, is likely to be one that has managed to reposition its staff resources within schools. Such close involvement will enable the provision of focused instrumental courses, as well as courses that initiate new areas of concern arising from everyday educational practice within the inner city. A current example of the latter might be a concern with the education of refugee children.

The third and final key activity relates to educational consultancy and research. A successful training institution will rest not only on its involvement in high quality training and professional development but also on the high quality of its consultancy work and research. In a successful training system, management and organisational structures will be in place to see research and teaching as of equal worth. A successful HEI concerned with education rests on this obvious foundation.

BIBLIOGRAPHY

Adey, P and Shayer, M (1994) *Cognitive Intervention and Academic Achievement*. London: Routledge

Anderson, B (1991) *Imagined Communities*. London: Verso

Baker, C (1988) *Key Issues in Bilingualism and Bilingual Education*. Clevedon: Multilingual Matters Ltd

Baside R (1965) *Sociologie des Maladies Mentales*. Paris: Flammarion

Bhabha, H (1990) 'Dissemiation: time, narrative, and the margins of the modern nation.' In Bhabha, H (Ed.), *Nation and Narration*. London: Routledge

Blum, J M (1978) *Pseudoscience and Mental Ability: The Origins and Fallacies of the IQ Controversy*. London: Monthly Review Press

Burke J(ed) *Competency Based Education and Training* Lewes: The Falmer Press

Bourdieu, P and Passeron, J C (1977) *Reproduction in Education, Society and Culture*. London: Sage

Camden Education Department (CLEA) (1991a): *Camden LEA Curriculum Statement*. London: CLEA

Camden Education Department (CLEA) (1991b): Mitchell, P *Letter to NQTs from Camden Director of Education*. London. CLEA

Camden Education Department, (1993) *Camden Articled Teacher Scheme Evaluation*. London: CLEA

Camden LEA (CLEA) (1996a) *Refugee Children in Camden Schools*, Statistics 1995 London: CLEA

Camden LEA (1996b) *Camden Refugee Education Policy: Developing a School Policy to meet the Educational Needs of Refugee Children: Draft Policy Framework for Schools*. London: CLEA

Camden LEA 1996c) *Asylum and Immigration Act: Key Proposals Update*. London: Camden Equalities Unit, CLEA

Capel, S, Leask M and Turner T (1996) *Learning to Teach in the Secondary School*. London and New York, Routledge

Carr, D (1993) 'Questions of Competence", *British Journal of Educational Studies* Vol 41, 1993, pg. 253-271

Castells, M (1977) *The Urban Question: a Marxist Approach*. London: Edward Arnold

Castells, M (1983) *The City and the Grassroots*. London: Edward Arnold

Centre for Multicultural Education (1992) *Sagaland: Youth Culture, Racism and Education: A Report on Research Carried out in Thamesmead*. London: London Borough of Greenwich

Charter, D (1996) 'Schools must not blur boundary of culture, says curriculum chief.' *The Times*, 8 February, 1996, p. 7

Collison, J (1994) in *The Times Educational Supplement*, 23rd September, 1994

Cooper, G (1995) 'Inner London 'most deprived part of Britain'.' *The Independent*, 10 November 1995, p. 6

Coulby, D, and Jones, C (1995) *Postmodernity and European Education Systems: Cultural Diversity and Centralist Knowledge*. Stoke-on-Trent: Trentham Books

DES (Department of Education and Science) (1978) *Special Educational Needs* (The Warnock Report) London: HMSO

DES (Department of Education and Science) and the Welsh Office (1985) *Education for All* (Swann Report) London: HMSO

DES (Department of Education and Science) (1988) *The New Teacher in School: a Survey by HM Inspectors in England and Wales, 1987*. London: HMSO

DES (Department of Education and Science) (1990) *The Treatment and Assessment of Probationary Teachers (Administrative Memorandum 1/90)*. London: HMSO

DES (Department of Education and Science) (1991) *Letter from Paul Long, Teacher Training Division to all LEAs in England*, 31 July 1991. London: DES

DES (Department of Education and Science) (1992) *The Induction and Probation of New Teachers, 1988-1991: A Report by HMI*. Ref. 62/92/NS. London: HMSO

DFE (Department for Education) and the Welsh Office (1992) *Initial Teacher Training (Secondary Phase)* Circular 9/92. London: HMSO

DFE (Department for Education) (1993a) *The Initial Training of Primary School Teachers: New Criteria for Courses Approval* (Circular, 14/93. London: HMSO

DFE (Department for Education) (1993b) *The Government's Proposals for the Reform of Initial Teacher Training*, E/EO 325/93, September 1993. London: HMSO

DFE (Department for Education) (1994a) *The Education of Children*, Circular 9/94. London. DFE

DFE (Department for Education) (1994b) *Code of Practice on the Identification and Assessment of Special Educational Needs*. London: DFE

DFE (Department for Education) and the Welsh Office (1995) *Information Technology in the National Curriculum* (London. HMSO 1995)

Department for Education Northern Ireland (1993) *Review of Initial Teacher Training (ITT) in Northern Ireland. Report of the Development Group (Working Group IV)*, Belfast: Department of Education Northern Ireland

Duckenfield, M (1995) Schools for Cities. OECD *Programme on Educational Building*. Paris: Organisation for Co-operation and Economic Development [OECD]

Earley, P (1992) *Beyond Initial Teacher Training: Induction and the Role of the LEA*. Slough: National Foundation for Educational Research (NFER)

Earley, P and Kinder, K (1994) *Initiation Rights: Effective Induction Practices for New Teachers*. Slough: NFER

Evans, B and Waites B (1981) *IQ and Mental Testing*. London: Macmillan

Findlay, R and Reynolds, J (eds) (1987) *Children from Refugee Communities: a Question of Identity: Uprooting, Integrating or Dual Culture?* Derby: Derby Refugee Action

Fullan, M, (1992) *The New Meaning of Educational Change*, London: Cassell

Furlong, J and Maynard, T (1995) *Mentoring Student Teachers: The Growth of Professional Knowledge*. London: Routledge

Gardiner J (1996a) 'Teacher training in school no panacea' in *Times Educational Supplement*. 19 July, 1996

Gardiner J (1996b) 'Staff training chief seeks lull in rhetoric.' *Times Educational Supplement*. 19 July, 1996

Garson S *et al.* (1990) *The World Languages Project*. London. Hodder Educational

Giroux, H (1992) 'Postmodernism and the discourse of educational criticism.' In Aronowitz, S and Giroux, H (Ed.) (1992) *Postmodern Education: Politics, Culture and Social Criticism.* London: University of Minnesota Press

Grace, G (1979) *Teachers, Ideology and Control.* London: Routledge and Kegan Paul

Griffiths, V and Owen, P (1995) *Schools in Partnership.* London: Paul Chapman Publishing

Hall, D (1995) *Assessing the Needs of Bilingual Children: Living in Two Languages.* London: David Fulton

Hall, S *et al.* (ed) (1992) *Modernity and its Futures.* Cambridge: Polity Press

Halsey, A H (1972) *Educational Priority, Volume. 1. EPA Problems and Policies.* London: HMSO

Halsey, A H *et al.* (1980) *Origins and Destinations.* Oxford: Oxford University Press

Hargreaves, D H *et al* (1984) *Improving Secondary Schools.* London: Inner London Education Authority

Harris, V (1993) 'Partners are people – relationships in partnership schemes' in Thorogood, J (ed.) (1993) *Partners: a Guide to School-based Initial Teacher Training in Modern Languages* London: CILT

Hester H (1988) 'Criteria for use in assessing English language development' in Barrs, M *et al.* *The Primary Language Handbook.* London: CILT

Hofkins, D (1994) 'Mentors 'ignored' trainees' in *Times Educational Supplement,* 2, Primary, 23 September, 1994

ILEA (Inner London Education Authority) (1989) *Prospects for Education in Inner London after 1990.* London: ILEA

Jensen, A R (1969) 'How Much Can We Boost IQ and Scholastic Achievement?', *Harvard Education Review,* 39

Jones, C (1992) 'Cities, diversity and education.' In Coulby, D and Jones, C (eds), *World Yearbook of Education 1992: Urban Education.* London: Kogan Page

Jones, C (1993) 'Refugee children in English urban schools.' *European Journal of Intercultural Studies,* 3(2/3), 29-40

Jones, C and Rutter, J (eds) (1998 forthcoming) *Mapping the Field: New Initiatives in Refugee Education.* Stoke-on-Trent: Trentham Books

Jones, K (1989) *Right Turn: The Conservative Revolution in Education.* London: Hutchinson Radius

Jones, J (1994) *Teacher as Reflective Professional [Occasional Paper in Teacher Education and Training.* London: Insitute of Education, London University

Kaplan, L and Edelfelt, R (1996) *Teachers for the New Millennium.* California: Corwin Press

Learmonth, J and Maidment, L (1993) *Teaching and Learning in Cities.* London: Whitbread

Levine, J (1981) 'Developing pedagogies for multilingual learners.' in *English in Education* 15 (3) p. 25-34

McDonald, D and Elias, D (1980): The Problems of beginning teachers: A Crisis in Training, quoted in Fullan, M, (1992) *The New Meaning of Educational Change.* London: Cassell

McBride R (Ed) (1996) *Teacher Education Policy* Lewes: Falmer Press

Mortimore, P *et al* (1988) *Schools Matters: The Junior Years.* Wells: Open Books

Mullard, C (1980) *Racism in Society and Schools: History, Policy and Practice.* London: University of London, Institute of Education

Mumford, L (1961) *The City in History.* London: Secker and Warburg

Murphy, P and Moon, B (1989) *Developments in Learning and Assessment.* London: Hodder and Stoughton

National Commission on Education (1993) *Learning to Succeed.* London: Heinemann

Ofsted (Office for Standards in Education) (1993a): *The New Teacher in School: A survey by HM Inspectors in England and Wales 1992.* London: HMSO

Ofsted (Office for Standards in Education) (1993b): *A Handbook for the Inspection of Schools* London: HMSO

The Open University (1994) *Postgraduate Certificate in Education Mentors Materials.* Milton Keynes: OU

Refugee Council (1989) *Teaching and Learning about Refugees: a Resource List.* London: Refugee Council

Refugee Council and World University Service (WUS) (1990) *Refugee Education in the 1990s* London: Refugee Council/ WUS

Rieck W (1992), 'The Current Undergraduate Pedagogical Preparation of Secondary School teachers.' Paper presented at the Annual Conference of the Mid-South Educational research Association (21st Knoxville, TN Nov. 11 – 13 1992)

Rutter, J (1994) *Refugee Children in the Classroom.* Stoke-on-Trent: Trentham Books

Rutter, M *et al.* (1979) *Fifteen Thousand Hours.* London: Open Books

Salmon, P (1980) *Coming to Know.* London: Routledge and Kegan Paul

Sammons, P (1994) 'Gender, Ethnic and Socio-Economic Differences in Attainment and Progress: A Longitudinal Analysis of Student Achievement over Nine Years". Paper given at Educational Research Association Annual Meeting, New Orleans, USA, 1994

Sammons, P *et al.* (1994a) *Continuity of School Effects: A Longitudinal Analysis of Primary and Secondary School Effects on GCSE Performance.* London: Mss, Department of Curriculum Studies, Institute of Education, University of London

Sammons, P *et al.* (1994b) *Assessing School Effectiveness: Developing Measures to put School Performance in Context.* London: Ofsted

Scarr, S (1984) *Race, Social Class and Individual Differences in IQ.* London: Lawrence Erlbaum

Schon, D (1983) *The Reflective Practitioner: How Professionals Think in Action.* New York: Basic Books

Stenhouse, L (1975) *An Introduction to Curriculum Research and Development.* London: Heinemann

Stenhouse, L (1983) *Authority, Education and Emancipation.* London: Heinemann

Stenhouse, L (ed) (1980) *Curriculum Research and Development in Action.* London: Heinemann

Street-Porter, R (1977) *Race, Children and Cities.* Milton Keynes: Open University Press

Surrey County Council and Roehampton Institute of Education (1993) *The New Teacher Competency Profile.* (Surrey Education Services, SES)

Tate, N (1996) 'Culture is not anarchy.' *The Times,* 8 February, 1996, p. 18

TTA (Teacher Training Agency) (1996) *National Standards for Teachers* [TTA News no. 11/96.] London: TTA

Thompson, M (1992): 'Do 27 competences make a teacher? Or, why chickens should decide the sauce in which they are to be served', in *Education Review,* Autumn 1992, pp. 4-7

Wagner, P and Lodge, C (eds) (1985) *Refugee Children in School.* London: National Association for Pastoral Care in Education

Warner, R (ed.) (!991a) *Voices From Kurdistan.* London: Minorities Rights Group

Warner, R (ed.) (!991b) *Voices From Uganda.* London: Minorities Rights Group

Watermann, S (1996) 'Between the Lines' *Guardian Education,* 16 January, 1996

Watkins, C (1992) An Experiment in Mentor Training in Wilkin, M (ed.) (1992)

Whitty G *et al.* (1992) 'Initial teacher training in England and Wales: a survey of current practices and concerns'. *Cambridge Journal of Education*, 22, 3, pp. 293-306

Wilkin, M (ed) (1992) *Mentoring in Schools.* London: Kogan Page

Wideen, M and Grimmett P, (eds), (1995) *Changing Times in Teacher Education, Restructuring or Reconceptualisation?* Lewes: Falmer Press

World University Service (WUS) (1995a) *Entitled to Learn: a Report on Young Refugees Experiences of Access and Progression in the UK Education System.* London: WUS

World University Service (WUS) (1995b) *Refugee Education Policy is Failing: Proposals for Change.* London: WUS

INDEX